THE DIVE RESCUE SPECIALIST TRAINING MANUAL

by Steven J. Linton, Damon A. Rust and T. Daniel Gilliam
with Liam F. Rooney

Published by Concept Systems, Inc.

ACKNOWLEDGEMENTS

The authors of this manual wish to thank the numerous divers and dive teams who contributed to this work. Helpful assistance was also received from Dr. Martin J. Nemiroff of the United States Coast Guard, Doug Kelly of the Larimer County Dive Rescue Team and Colorado State University Department of Anthropology, Cpl. R. G. Teather of the Royal Canadian Mounted Police, Dr. Michael Charney of the Colorado State University Lab for Human Identification, and Dale Bergstrom of Poudre Valley Hospital in Fort Collins, Colorado.

TABLE OF CONTENTS

INTRODUCTION

The purpose of this manual is to take the romance and bravado out of underwater rescue and recovery operations. To some, the work of a Dive Rescue Specialist appears to be more a test of courage than simply another aspect of emergency service. However, since 1977 Dive Rescue Inc./International has taught that this perception can hamper a dive team's safety and effectiveness.

Dive calls often do involve physical danger and emotionally-charged situations. But the fine line between success and failure, which frequently translates to the difference between life and death, requires a no-frills professionalism on the part of every individual on the dive team.

The modern rescue diver is trained and equipped with skills and values different from his contemporaries in sport diving. While the sport diver looks for ideal diving conditions (clear visibility, warm, calm water), the rescue diver is inevitably called to dive under the worst of conditions. Dive team members must be able to work effectively in zero visibility waters. They often dive in inclement weather or face the risk of entanglement with such hazards as bottom debris or vehicles underwater.

For these reasons, dive team members must keep certain aspects in the forefront of their minds throughout every operation. Respect of such operational terms as the Risk/Benefit Factor, Rescue Mode, Recovery Mode, and the Predive Checklist can have a direct effect on the well-being of the divers operating under negative conditions. Similarly, the proper use of such factors will make the difference between a competent dive team and one that is run in the "management-by-crisis" style.

The Dive Rescue Specialist's role requires one to be constantly aware of the needs of the other dive team members. Rescue divers must be able to honestly assess their own limitations.

Underwater rescue and recovery work has advanced significantly in the last decade. Today, professional dive teams are just that — professional in performance and appearance, and continually giving their respective communities a high level of measurable service.

Successful dive team operations, particularly those involving the saves of cold-water near-drowning victims, have drawn praise and recognition from the media and the general public, thus raising public awareness and expectations. For example, today there is a proliferation of lawsuits arising out of cases where contemporary rescue techniques were not deployed. Advanced techniques and equipment have also raised the standards of emergency service agencies, which have a legal obligation to provide updated training and equipment to their employees.

Prior to organizing the dive team, an agency, department or volunteer group must assess the needs of their region and contact the authorities charged with local rescue operations. An effective team must be recognized by those responsible for public safety. The potential dive team must also assess the types of water, conditions, and accidents characteristic of their community. Without such preliminary footwork, the dive team is little more than a social club with no real direction or objectives.

Too often, a well-intentioned but poorly trained and equipped dive team will suffer public ridicule when they fail to perform a basic operation. The most straightforward dive call can completely overwhelm the untrained team before the eyes of the entire community. In such cases, the taxpayers are painfully aware of these shortcomings when they compare the local services with underwater units in other areas.

However, awareness by the public and local safety agencies has helped many competent teams receive the necessary support for equipment and training through a variety of avenues. Several factors have contributed to this awareness: Advances in emergency medicine for dealing with cold-water near-drowning victims have increased a dive team's life-saving potential. The increased popularity of water sports has put more people in or near the water. And law enforcement agencies are becoming increasingly aware of the potential for recovering evidence lost or concealed underwater.

There are currently some all-volunteer dive teams in the United States that have been able to raise large annual budgets — the result of demonstrating a high level of service to their respective communities. A well-coordinated dive team within a fire or police department will likewise win the respect of its administration.

Once you have established the purpose of your dive team, it is time to design an approach to constructing an effective force of divers. Selection, training and equipment priorities must be planned as carefully as any dive team operation. This manual is designed to take the guesswork out of all aspects of dive team training and operations.

Dive Rescue Inc./International has influenced the procedures and policies of thousands of agencies and departments throughout North America. The popularity of Dive Rescue training is due to the source of the information presented in this manual — real life situations. Dive Rescue trainers are all former fulltime law enforcement or fire service personnel who have served on numerous underwater rescue and recovery operations.

The Dive Rescue Specialist Training Manual is the result of not only our own field operations but of our experiences in training thousands of rescue divers who are operating throughout the world. Graduates of Dive Rescue programs include members of local, state and federal agencies from all over the North American continent and public safety divers in Australia and Europe. The success of the dive teams these individuals represent can be attributed to proper preparation, training and the right attitude.

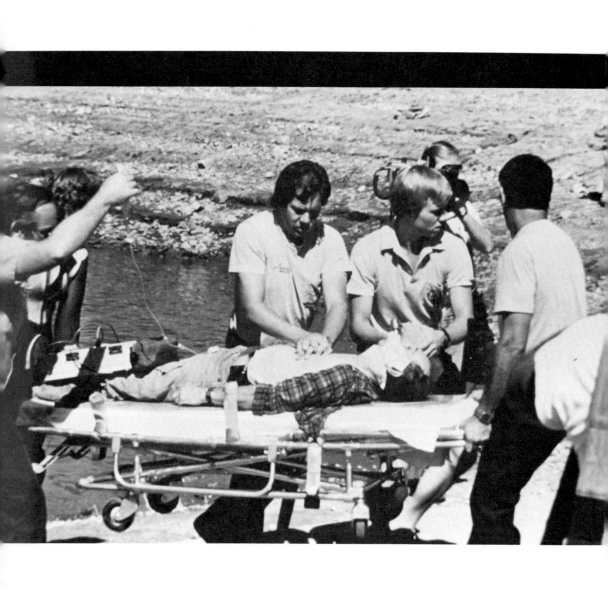

DROWNING ACCIDENTS

Drowning is the bottom line of underwater rescue and recovery work — it is the reason most individuals and departments are involved with this profession. In both the United States and Canada, drowning is the second leading cause of accidental death of persons between the ages of one and forty-four. Together, the two countries average 8,500 drowning deaths each year.

The Dive Rescue Specialist must have a basic understanding of drowning accidents and the approach to treating victims to be an effective dive team member. Such skills are important even though the most practical arrangement separates the role of the dive team and the paramedics — the diver delivers the victim to the paramedics who are the specialists in resuscitation procedures.

There are some teams whose members will include local emergency medical technicians, paramedics, or even doctors. Effective dive teams are closely linked with the medical staffs in their community by consistently exchanging information and participating in joint training exercises. Everyone's effectiveness is enhanced when the challenges of the various tasks and responsibilities are understood by all involved.

In less than ideal situations, the emergency medical orientation of a dive team has helped save lives despite the lack of awareness of professionals in certain regions. For example, in the past several years there have been at least two incidents where dive team members have had to convey the potential of resuscitation to emergency medical teams. In both instances the victims were completely resuscitated — victims that otherwise would have been declared dead.

Fortunately, the growing awareness of the cold-water near-drowning phenomena has inspired the majority of medical professionals to persist in resuscitation efforts beyond the outdated time limits employed for so many years. In fact, there are some communities where progressive emergency medical teams have been hampered by the inability of the local police or fire departments to retrieve victims out of the water quickly enough.

The relationship between a dive team and the local medical community will be discussed in greater detail in Chapter Four. Regardless of interagency arrangements, however, the rescue diver must understand the physiology of drowning and the basic components of resuscitating the victims likely to be found in the water.

The Physiology of Drowning

Drowning is generally defined as any death caused by submersion in the water. Of course, not all accidental deaths which occur in the water are due to drowning — although that is usually the assumption. Many times the cause of death may be trauma, heart failure or a number of other ailments. A victim drowns when he or she is suffocated by water intake through the mouth and into the lungs.

Wet vs. Dry Drowning

The majority of drowning victims (70 to 85 percent) succumb to a "wet drowning," or a drowning where water has filled the lungs thus stopping the ability to breath. Approximately 15 to 30 percent of drowning victims, however, succumb to a "dry drowning," or a drowning whereby the first gulp of cold water will cause a spasm of the larynx which subsequently suffocates the victim without flooding the lungs.

Initial treatment of victims of either condition does not vary as the lungs will quickly absorb the fresh water into the bloodstream and water from the stomach is normally vomited out. The primary objective of immediate CPR efforts is to establish an airway and send oxygen into the bloodstream.

Cold-Water Near-Drowning

The possiblity of saving the life of a person who has been submerged in water for a period of time puts that victim in another classification — the "near-drowning victim."

There are a variety of factors involved in the phenomena of cold-water near-drowning.

The most widely publicized factor contributing to cold-water near-drowning has been a physiological trait of sea mammals, the Mammalian Diving Reflex. The publicity surrounding the survival of infants and young children as a result of this reflex has dramatized the potential for saving lives of victims submerged for extended periods of time under one hour.

However, recent research points to a variety of other factors, the most prominent of which is general hypothermia, contributing to survival of the cold-water near-drowning victim.

The study of cold-water near-drowning is still relatively new — most research and public awareness began in the late 1970s — and theories regarding causes and treatment of cold-water near-drowning cases continue to be subjects of controversy. In light of the need for additional research and evidence, the dive team member must keep an open mind towards new findings.

Hypothermia

Hypothermia is generally defined as the condition of having one's body temperature fall below normal. The term is also used to describe the overall effects of severe cold on a victim. This refers to exposure to cold temperatures either in the water, topside, or both.

It is believed that hypothermia contributes to the survival of cold-water near-drowning victims in that the condition greatly reduces the body's need for oxygen. Through the slowing down of blood circulation to tissues, muscles and non-vital organs, blood is channeled to the essential organs of the heart, lungs and brain.

A Life Is Saved

When the family car rolled into Carter Lake, 5 year old Justin was trapped inside. Within 25 minutes, the youngster had been pulled from the submerged car by divers who battled chilly water and zero visibility. After aggressive resuscitation efforts at the scene by paramedics, Justin was rushed by air ambulance to a medical facility.

One month later, a fully-recovered Justin honored the heroic divers who had saved his life. Without their efforts and the cooperation of many agencies, Justin's tale would have ended in tragedy at the depths of Carter Lake.

The Mammalian Diving Reflex

When an air-breathing mammal, such as a whale or a porpoise, dives beneath the water's surface its general physiology changes in a way that is distantly similar to aspects of extreme hypothermia in humans. The breathing stops and blood is shunted away from nonessential tissues and directed to vital organs.

In humans the Mammalian Diving Reflex is believed to be triggered when the opthalmic branch of the fifth cranial nerve (which is located in the forehead and nasal regions) is immersed in cold water. This response is so consistent in slowing the heart rate that a medical report recently recommended the facial immersion of tachycardia patients (suffering accelerated heart rate) for 15 to 20 seconds while breathing through a snorkel.

In drowning accidents, the Mammalian Diving Reflex is much more pronounced in toddlers and young children than it is in older victims. However, this is not to say that older victims do not hold the potential for resuscitation after extended periods of submersion. The Mammalian Diving Reflex will likely be accompanied by other responses such as hypothermia, to cause the cold-water near-drowning syndrome.

While a sea mammal continues with its conscious activities while employing this reflex, the human drowning victim will give a convincing appearance of death: A near-drowning victim will not breathe, will have a pale or bluish color of skin, muscle rigidity, fixed and dilated pupils, and a pulse either absent or so slow that it is barely, if at all, detectable. As breathing ceases, the heart rate may stop or slow dramatically (as low as four to eight beats per minute) while a higher pressure blood flow is channeled to the heart, lungs and brain to compensate for the loss of oxygen caused by the drowning and subsequent lack of air.

Concerns for Brain Damage

For years, physicians have believed that any victim that could be resuscitated after four to six minutes underwater, would inevitably suffer irreversible brain damage. While brain damage is still a risk in the survivability of near-drowning victims, the high number of successful recoveries disputes the earlier preconceptions.

Currently, no statistics are kept on the incidence of cold-water near-drowning saves. However, rescue professionals everywhere are familiar with the steady increase of cases where victims have been rescued, revived and completely recovered after extended periods of up to 60 minutes underwater.

While the majority of these cases involve young victims in cold, clean waters, there have been cold-water near-drowning saves of victims with ages in the 60s. Cold-water near-drowning victims have been retrieved from polluted waters and from waters as warm as 70 degrees Fahrenheit.

Because there are so many variables involved in the cold-water near-drowning phenomena, and the research is continuously bringing new theories and evidence to light, the dive team member must take special care not to claim expertise outside of his or her own field — which is specifically victim retrieval.

Emergency Care for the Cold-Water Near-Drowning Victim

The treatment of cold-water near-drowning victims is a relatively new field. The myriad of factors an emergency room physician must deal with when attempting to save a near-drowning victim calls for an individual approach to every case.

The information presented here is only the tip of the iceberg of what is involved in treating such victims. Our purpose here is not to offer any hard and fast guidelines but to illustrate the general approach and innovations being used by some of the more progressive medical teams.

CPR

It is imperative that CPR efforts commence immediately. The effectiveness of the CPR administered to a victim is often the determining factor for survival.

Rescuers will want to watch for the inevitable gastric distension and vomiting which follows water aspiration. Be ready to clear the air passage before and during CPR. Do not, however, worry about getting water out of the victim's lungs. It's far more important to get oxygen into the lungs.

Logically, CPR administered on a hard surface is going to be more effective than CPR given by in-water techniques. Some believe in-water CPR has the additional risk of a rescuer inadvertently forcing gastric contents from the victim's stomach back down into the lungs because of the problems of establishing an airway. Only as a very last resort should the rescuer administer in-water CPR.

Airways, IVs and Transportation

Airway management is a critical aspect of CPR. The major post-resuscitation complication is the development of pneumonia, which is invariably caused by pollution of the airway with the victim's gastric contents.

If rescuers are trained and experienced in inserting artificial airways, they should do so at the scene, but only if it can be done without delay. Starting IVs at the scene, however, should not take priority over transporting the victim to the nearest medi-

cal facility. During transport of the patient, aggressive CPR should continue with the highest possible percentage of pure oxygen administered to the victim.

Rewarming

Rewarming of the victim should be done from the inside out. Do not use external techniques to rewarm the victim, such as rubbing to increase the circulation in the victim's extremities. Such techniques may flood the lungs and heart with cold, stagnant blood — blood that may be highly acidic and contain dangerous levels of toxic metabolites.

Rescuers may cover the victim's torso lightly to prevent further heat loss. Some emergency teams use full cocoon type bags which absorb water and shelter the victim while providing access for CPR and other treatment. But many teams still choose to leave the victim's legs and arms uncovered to prevent premature blood circulation.

Many teams carry portable apparatus for introducing heated oxygen into the victim's lungs. Heated oxygen can facilitate rewarming the heart. Since the lungs jacket the heart, they serve as effective heat exchangers, thus heating the heart very quickly when breathing warm air.

Body temperature readings are a high priority in treating cold-water near-drowning victims. A low-reading (down to 70 degrees Fahrenheit) thermometer is necessary. A flexible probe that can be fed down the esophagus to heart level is best for accurately monitoring the heart temperature. A rectal thermometer is less than ideal because it will record a much lower temperature long after the heart has begun to rewarm.

The emergency room physician will want to monitor body temperature in order to determine when it is safe to restart the heart. The heart must be rewarmed to at least 90 degrees Fahrenheit prior to restarting attempts such as defibrillation.

Upon arrival at the emergency room, the rescue or emergency medical team should supply the attending physician with water temperature, length of submersion time, the victim's approximate age and other possible injuries, as well as other vital statistics — such as any success they have had so far in raising the victim's core temperature.

Hospital Care of the Cold-Water Near-Drowning Victim

Successful dive teams often perform joint training sessions with the local emergency medical services and hospital staffs. An awareness of the challenges and obstacles faced by the medical teams treating the rescued victim will increase the dive team's effectiveness.

At the hospital, care should be directed to two critical areas: The rewarming of the heart and normalizing of the acid-base levels of the blood. This is best gauged by monitoring the arterial blood gases and EKG.

The inhalation of heated and humidified oxygen is one method of heating the body core. Such an approach will heat the brain and the heart before other parts of the body, thus minimizing the complications a victim may experience in rewarming. Part of an emergency medical team's preplanning for the treatment of near-drowning victims should include a means for providing heated oxygen. If a humidifier is used, oxygen should be heated to 105 to 108 degrees Fahrenheit.

Arterial oxygen partial pressure should be normalized to between 60 and 90 millimeters of mercury. In most cases, the medical staff will have to employ endotracheal intubation coupled with positive end expiratory pressure, which helps to reduce pulmonary edema and thus improves oxygen exchange.

Mechanical ventilators may be impractical as CPR interferes with their use. Thus, an ambu bag, or air bag, using 100 percent oxygen at 100 percent relative humidity, should be used for ventilation. Endotracheal intubation is usually necessary in near-

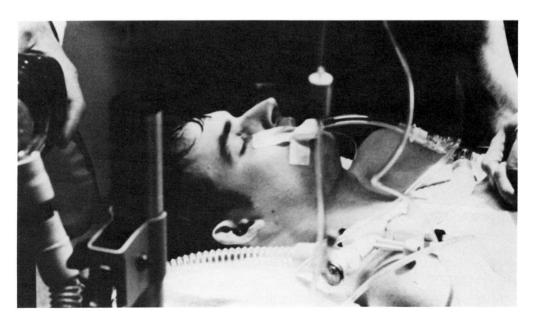

drowning cases, and should be followed by serial measurements of arterial blood gases.

Normalizing the acid-base levels of the blood is a high priority. Cold-water near-drowning patients usually have a low blood pH. If the patient's blood is highly acidic, administration of sodium bicarbonate solution should be considered, but acid-base levels improve quickly if circulation is reinstituted.

Since inhalation rewarming heats the myocardium quickly, the medical staff can usually apply electroshock defibrillation within minutes to stimulate a full heartbeat. Again, the heart must be rewarmed first (to at least 90 degrees Fahrenheit) otherwise it could be damaged by repeated defibrillatory shocks.

The general rule of thumb that most advanced medical staffs follow today is: Do not declare a cold patient dead. Resuscitation efforts should continue at least until a near normal body temperature has been approached. In short, efforts should not cease until the patient is rewarmed and still shows no response to resuscitation — which could take hours.

During hospital treatment of the near-drowning patient, chest X-rays should be taken to assess the status of the lungs. Also, intensive monitoring of cardiac output and measures of ventilation perfusion or intra-pulmonary shunting are essential.

Lab studies should include arterial blood gases, electrolytes, blood urea nitrogen, creatinine, serum hemoglobin and clotting profile.

Not infrequently, near-drowning victims have been successfully resuscitated only to succumb later to complications. Initial and subsequent lab studies are designed to prevent such circumstances. The medical staff should be particularly watchful for acute respiratory distress syndrome, acute renal failure, hemolysis, and diffuse intravascular coagulation.

The Dive Team's Role in Treatment

Of course, no amount of emergency medicine or sophisticated hospital techniques will help until the victim is retrieved from the water. The latest findings of Dr. Martin Nemiroff and his colleagues place a great responsibility upon the local dive team.

In some regions of the country, this responsibility has already been translated to liability: If a victim is not retrieved as quickly as possible then the public will question the level of service their local safety agencies are providing.

Should the dive team suspect that local physicians and other medical staff are not receptive to the potential for saving the lives of cold-water near-drowning victims, they may seek to change attitudes through a public information campaign. Various sources for educational materials can provide assistance. For additional information contact the International Association of Dive Rescue Specialists, 2619 Canton Court, Fort Collins, CO 80525, (303) 482-0887.

Summary

Underwater rescue operations can offer the most rewarding opportunities a dive team will ever face. Each year, an increasing number of dive teams and medical professionals are combining forces to accomplish feats considered impossible less than a decade ago. Victims of all ages are being retrieved from a wide variety of submersion situations to be completely resuscitated and allowed to continue leading normal, productive lives.

The Dive Rescue Specialist and his or her dive team must be trained and equipped to respond to this increased demand for lifesaving service.

SELECTING, TRAINING AND EQUIPPING THE DIVE RESCUE SPECIALIST

A dive team is only as good as its individual divers and their ability to function as a team. The selection of individual members, training and equipment are major focal points in developing the dive team. From the onset, the dive team must establish the values and policies which become basic standards for operation. Whether the team is just being organized or has been in existence for a number of years, attention to the selection process, proper training and proper equipment contribute to the safety of the individual divers and the level of their service to the community.

Selecting the Dive Rescue Specialist

A dive team can prevent many problems by carefully screening potential members. When evaluating a candidate the most significant factor is the individual's attitude.

Dive team leaders and administrators should examine the motives and history of applicants. Psychologists involved with dive teams and other aspects of emergency service note that a motive such as the need for stimulating work is not necessarily unfavorable.

However, the individual who emphatically professes a number of high ideals, or exhibits a need to become a hero, should be considered very cautiously. The individual who particularly demonstrates a tendency towards the hero role may have problems with team work. Such individuals often don't make good heroes either: They often suffer poor judgement inspired by self-seeking motives during operations.

Many dive teams require their diving candidates to pass physical fitness tests. Swimming and basic water safety should be a part of such exams. The candidate should demonstrate a reasonable amount of ease and comfort in and around the water. This is not to say that the potential dive team member must already be a certified diver. Often, it is easier to start with one who has had no diving experience at all — making it easier to standardize skills among the divers.

Most dive teams fill their ranks with the members of other local emergency service units (i.e. police and fire departments). However, many good dive teams are completely volunteer, or have capable volunteers working alongside local emergency service professionals.

While professional law enforcement and

fire service personnel are usually the most experienced in dealing with stress and emergencies, it is the individual, not the rank nor the departmental affiliation, that should be considered.

Sample Interview Questions of the Dive Team Candidate

The dive team should conduct a relatively formal interview of all candidates — diving and non-diving. While the atmosphere should not be intimidating, it should convey the seriousness of the interview. Also, a mild pressure situation such as a small panel of interviewers could provide hints to the candidate's personality.

Following are some examples of interview questions that could be helpful in evaluating a candidate:

1) How would you define teamwork?
2) Why are you a good team worker?
3) What will you gain personally from being a dive team member?
4) Are you available and willing to train with the team even though you are not being paid to do so?
5) Are you available for dive calls that may come at any time, day or night?
6) How do you deal with situations involving death or dead bodies?
7) Give some examples of stressful situations that you have handled.
8) How does your family feel about you being on the dive team?
9) Do you get along well with others?
10) Do you have any diving experience? If so, describe it.
11) What sort of high school or college sports did you participate in? Hobbies or pastimes?
12) Why should you be accepted on the dive team?

Medical Requirements

Dive team candidates should be required to pass a medical exam administered by a doctor familiar with diving medicine. Particular caution should be made when considering potential members with respiratory, heart or blood pressure problems. A physician with a good background in diving medicine can help assure a careful and reasoned approach to the team's medical standards.

Physical Conditioning

The dive team should have physical requirements for diving members at both the entry level and on a re-evaluation basis. Swimming abilities are often a natural focus. A diver's comfort with the water environment, as well as his or her aerobic condition, can effectively be gauged through a simple swimming test.

The dive team should not, however, overemphasize the physical aspects of the individual dive team member. While team members should be physically capable of holding their own during an operation, such factors as team spirit and mental attitude should be weighed more heavily than physical prowess. The dive team's physical fitness requirements should be realistic. Excessively strenuous physical requirements could be self-defeating.

However, a diving member should be in better physical condition than the average person as this profession will require physical exertion under stressful situations at times. Divers must take the initiative to keep themselves in top physical condition through a regular exercise regimen.

Mental Preparation

Mental conditioning is essential to preparing the dive team member to be of maximum service to the team and the public. Attention to this aspect of preparation helps the diver handle the inherent stress of this line of work.

There are many misconceptions about stress. A common fallacy is that stress can be reduced through physical activity. While physical exertion, as through an aggressive game of racquetball, does seem to relieve tension, research has shown that such releases do not actually minimize stress. Nor do they enable the individual to deal with stressful situations as they occur. Such activities are important for physical conditioning of the dive team member, but other avenues are suggested for dealing with stress factors.

Psychotherapists today recommend body relaxation techniques and team debriefings as conventional approaches to dealing with stress. Many therapy professionals are also suggesting unconventional methods, such as prayer and meditation, for addressing stress. Whatever approach the dive team takes, stress should be dealt with in advance. The diver who is conditioned to operate under stressful situations will be much more effective in the field than the one who is not.

Training the Individual Diver

The training and preparation of a dive team is approached on two levels: The training of the individual diver and the development of a coordinated team. Often, these two levels will overlap, as they should: A good dive team is composed of competent divers who operate as emergency service professionals both topside and underwater.

Each member must be able to think for himself and to act asssertively and, in some situations, independently if he encounters trouble underwater. At the same time, that individual must be a team player at all times. This is not a contradiction in terms, but a quality needed in demanding and often dangerous operations where communications are limited, with low or zero visibility a frequent factor, and numerous unpredictable factors.

Naturally, scuba skills are the first priority in training a dive team member. A good diver will be able to acquire such skills as running search patterns much more easily than a diver who is still struggling with his own inexperience in the water. However, the most promising team member is not necessarily the veteran diver. Often it is easier and simpler to train a dive team from scratch than it is to try to change old habits or conform the methods of divers with a variety of diving backgrounds. The degree of difficulty in the latter situation depends, of course, upon the attitudes of the divers involved.

Again, the dive team MUST be comprised of good divers. A simple working definition of a "good diver" is one with a comfortable skill level. No matter what diving experience a candidate has, it is wise to run each potential member through a basic skills class. Likewise, veteran members should have their basic scuba skills reviewed through a regular recertification process implemented by the dive team.

Teamwork is the bottom line of every operation. Each individual diver and topside member must be conditioned to respond, even when making an individual response, with the same logic and actions as his or her colleagues.

For example, if 20 dive team members are asked to write down the procedure for responding to a "need help" signal (transmitted to a line tender from a diver underwater) there should be 20 identical answers written down.

To effect this uniformity, the dive team members practice in regular pool and open water training sessions. Constant research and education should update the dive team's skills and broaden its service to the community.

The individual Dive Rescue Specialist should possess the following basic scuba skills:
- Dressing and equipment handling
- Entries
- Kicks
- Snorkeling (with and without mask)
- BC work (on surface)
- Surface dives
- Clearing ears
- Regulator breathing (no mask)
- Mask clearing
- Regulator clearing (three ways)
- Controlled descent
- Buoyancy control (underwater)
- Swimming ascent
- Buddy breathing (with and without mask)
- Sharing air ascent (with and without octopus)
- Emergency ascent

Training the Dive Team

Human nature permits a tendency to become complacent at one level of expertise. For the Dive Rescue Specialist, and the community he serves, such complacency is dangerous. The rescue diver is never finished training as long as he holds his certification.

The dive team must coordinate a system of training, recertification and record keeping to maintain the members' performance levels. Many dive teams often hold monthly training sessions, usually with both classroom and open water sessions. Such training sessions can be held to a one or two day schedule depending upon the specific intent.

As a community's environment changes with the seasons, so should the dive team's focus change. For example: In the spring, prepare for swiftwater calls on the local rivers. In the summer, boating and deep diving skills are emphasized for lake and ocean calls. Dive calls in autumn months may involve searches in the weed infested marshes

The DIVE RESCUE SPECIALIST TRAINING SYSTEM includes the Dive Rescue Specialist Certificate, the Diver Training Record, the Dive Rescue I Skills Update and the Datalog.

frequented by hunters. Winter calls inevitably will require training and equipment preparations for dealing with ice and frigid water, in many parts of the country.

Interagency training is especially beneficial. For example, training with the local paramedics will greatly enhance a victim's chances during a rescue; joint training with local law enforcement can facilitate evidence searches; etc.

The dive team should pursue training with tow trucks, helicopters, watercraft and other additional equipment. The time to become oriented to the needs and workings of the different apparatus is before, not during, the actual operation.

Training sessions should be interesting and stimulating exercises. The dive team

should also seek out opportunities to tap the expertise of local equipment manufacturers, dealers, therapists (stress counseling), law enforcement (i.e. witness interviewing presentations) and fire service professionals (i.e. hazardous materials orientation).

The team should appoint one person who is responsible for logging each member's bottom times, training participation and recertifications. In addition to formal training sessions, the dive team may consider a requirement of a certain amount of diving time every 30 to 60 days. Recertifications should be held annually for ALL dive team members. Normally, most recertification can be handled in a one or two day session involving both open water and classroom reviews of skills and procedures.

As a unit, the dive team should possess the following basic skills:
- First responder techniques for cold-water near-drowning
- Team organization and leadership
- Scene evaluation
- Handling of the victim's family, witnesses and media
- Search patterns
- Victim retrieval (Rescue and Recovery Modes)
- Retrieval of submerged vehicles
- Evidence recovery and preservation
- Awareness of the physiology of body refloat

Specialty skills that a dive team develops will depend upon the types of water and the topography of their respective region. Some of these speciality skills may include:
- Swiftwater rescue and recovery
- Ice rescue and diving
- Vertical access work
- Helicopter use
- Lift work (refloating objects)
- Dealing with contaminated water
- Use of surface supply air systems

Dive Team Organization and Leadership

It is imperative that all dive team members respect and recognize the dive team leadership. Without this important relationship between the divers, tenders, other support personnel and the dive team leaders, effective and organized operations are virtually impossible.

The first step to establishing dive team leadership is recognizing the different roles between a leader and the divers. The competent dive team leader will resist the temptation to suit up and plunge into the water. It is the team leader's responsibility to maintain constant control while overseeing the entire operation from topside. The team leader's top priority is the safety of all dive team members. He oversees and/or delegates coordination with the media, other agencies, the use of manpower and the procurement of equipment.

In some instances, a poor leader may be a good diver. And when the pressure of an operation increases, this person will often want to revert to the role in which he is the most comfortable — jumping into the water and abandoning his topside command post. Such situations are an invitation for trouble.

A tragic example of this occurred when the dive team leader of a small town police department donned his gear and dove into a lake — leaving his team leaderless during an operation. The team leader/diver ran into problems, but there was no one on shore to direct a backup procedure. Subsequently, the team leader drowned while his dive team, helpless through their lack of direction, watched from shore.

The dive team leader must maintain a firm hand on the situation and his divers' performance. Yet he should be accessible and receptive to input from the team members. A closed-minded team leader could quickly evolve into an obstacle that the team members will be trying to work around rather than with. In short, the team leader's skills and actions must provide the team with support and direction. The team leader is a resource as well as an authority.

The Professional Image

Whether the Dive Rescue Specialist is a paid or volunteer member of an underwater rescue and recovery unit, he or she should strive to exhibit professionalism both in and out of the field. Professionalism is often defined as the quality of possessing the skills of a given profession. It also denotes a high level of specialized training, skill and ethical standards.

Dive team members and their families must always be aware of how they are presenting the team's image. The diver's outward appearance makes the first impression at the scene. Therefore, when answering a call, members of some teams find it convenient to quickly don the team uniform of coveralls or jumpsuits, with an identifying patch, and matching cap over whatever clothing they may be wearing at the time. Members should avoid showing up at the scene in such clothing as novelty T-shirts, cut-offs, or sloppy dress.

Quiet mannerisms on the job will not only help to minimize confusion at the scene, but also help to streamline communications among team members. Communications should be handled as subtly as possible, opting for radio communications and hand signals over shouting or loud conversations.

Horseplay has no place at the scene of a dive operation and should not be tolerated among team members.

During a long, drawn-out operation, the team leader must be aware of how the actions of the dive team may impress others present. For example, if divers are exhausted and need to relax it is often best to send them to another location, such as in the dive truck or back to the station house, rather than having them nap under a tree while the victim's family stands nearby waiting for the body recovery operation to continue.

Consideration of the impression being made on others at the scene and elsewhere will benefit the dive team's relations with the family, public, media and other agencies. Thus, the dive team's overall effectiveness and service to the community is enhanced.

A Measurable Level of Service

The professional image is composed of more than the appearance and mannerisms of the dive team. Most teams are dependent upon funding from a variety of sources, such as the local sheriff's department, fire department, other emergency services, and fund-raising activities through the public and private sectors. The dive team must demonstrate resourceful use of funds and manpower, and provide a measurable level of service to the community. In addition to its lifesaving potential, a dive team can demonstrate its ability to function as an underwater salvage unit, quick response unit for catastrophes such as flooding, and an aid to local law enforcement authorities.

In response to public awareness of cold-water near-drowning, a competent dive team can protect a department, and thus the municipal government and subsequently the taxpayers, from the not uncommon liability cases which arise out of poor responses to drowning scenarios.

Meticulous documentation of operations, team training and expenditures are the marks of a team with an effective, business-like administration. Slide shows and presentations for the public and outside agencies help educate others to the dive team's operational needs and capabilities. Always remember that the dive team is viewed by many as an elite force and that public expectations are high. The dive team that receives support from its community and the related local agencies has no doubt earned it.

Equipment

Too often, the efforts of a competent dive team or an individual diver are limited by inadequate or defective equipment during a crucial phase of an operation. As with skill, the success or failure of many operations often hinges on one small detail.

The professional dive team should not only have the best trained divers in their locale, they should also be the best equipped.

The dive team's ability to convince the pertinent authorities to include them in the budget largely depends upon the team's image and performance.

Knowledge and ability in handling scuba and special rescue equipment will only come through hours of practice both topside and in the water. Divers should not find themselves pulling old equipment out of the locker that has not been seen, let alone handled, since the last operation.

If the dive team is working as an effective emergency service in its community, then it can overcome the problems of expense and politics and see that its divers are well-equipped before undertaking an operation.

Standardization

Marginal or inadequate equipment can cost lives. It is imperative that divers at least have their own set of basic scuba gear. Each set should include mask, fins and snorkel, an environmentally protected regulator, an octopus regulator, a pressure gauge, a buoyancy control device with an auto inflator, weight belt and a knife. Also, each diver should have thermal protection, a wet suit or a dry suit, adequate for the temperatures in the dive team's region. When dealing with contaminated waters, a dry suit is recommended.

All equipment among dive team members should be identical (with the exception of personal items such as mask, fins and snorkel). Such standardization of scuba gear helps to promote identical procedures among individual divers underwater. In emergencies, it is much easier for divers to help one another when they are familiar with each other's equipment.

Also, it is more convenient to stock spare parts for scuba gear when every diver uses the same brands and models of equipment. Each diver should have his or her own complete set of scuba gear already fitted and ready for deployment during an operation.

Non-divers should wear PFDs (personal flotation devices) whenever near the water during any training or field operation. In addition to being a necessary safety precaution, such use of PFDs by the dive team's topside personnel serves as a good example to the general public. PFDs should meet standards approved by the United States Coast Guard. Ideally, the PFDs should be adjustable so they can be worn by a variety of people.

Updated Equipment

Despite the research and advances of modern scuba diving, too many underwater rescue and recovery divers are diving without such essentials as buoyancy control devices, pressure and depth gauges, and octopus regulators.

A Dive Rescue Specialist should have the following basic equipment:
- Mask
- Fins
- Snorkel
- Knives (one for high attachment and one for low attachment, in the event of entanglement)
- Regulator
- Pressure Gauge
- Alternate Air Source
- Buoyancy Compensator with Power Inflator
- Thermal Protection adequate for environment (wet/dry suit)
- Depth Gauge
- Compass
- Watch
- Tank
- Weight Belt

Dive teams should avoid the use of out-dated equipment. For example, many dive teams have replaced J-valves on tanks with K-valves, which cannot be accidentally altered to misrepresent a diver's air supply. A small number of divers still believe the use of a J-valve negates the necessity of a pressure gauge. However, J-valves can malfunction and have cost rescue divers their lives.

Pressure gauges are also a subject of controversy at times. Despite the visibility factor of the water, a diver will always benefit from the use of a pressure gauge. As will be explained in a later chapter, the gauge is used topside, as well as underwater, to monitor the diver's air supply. Likewise, there is often a debate regarding the superiority of "stab jackets" over the cheaper, but outdated, horsecollar-style buoyancy control devices.

Serviceability

Top quality equipment should be selected. Higher quality equipment will save money over the long term with fewer repair costs and less down time. When purchasing equipment the dive team should research the availability of service (repair and parts). Look for a well-reputed manufacturer, preferably one that is within easy shipping distance or has nearby local outlets.

Avoid in-house servicing of scuba equipment. Divers should not service their own equipment, unless they are certified by the manufacturer to do so, for reasons of safety and liability.

Summary

While diving is a technical, equipment-intensive skill, the human element is where problems often arise. Thus, screening candidates, training and the maintenance of skills become major concerns for the dive team. A dive team must never become an exclusive group. Membership should never be based upon gender, race, color or creed. However, no member should be admitted without a careful and realistic evaluation. To allow an individual who is unsuited for the work on the dive team would be a disservice to that candidate, the team and the public it serves — it could also be a fatal mistake.

The objectives of training and recertification must be kept in focus at all times. Dive team participation is not a competitive sport. The purpose of documenting performance is to encourage the improvement of skills — not to award prestige.

Equipping the dive team is a gradual, ongoing process. Proper equipment of good quality is essential when considering the dive team's safety and effectiveness. Most dive teams operate under financial constraints which could serve as barriers to receiving reliable equipment. However, because of the critical nature of equipment in the underwater environment, many teams have employed a great deal of ingenuity and creativity to seek various avenues of funding. Public education, community involvement, private sector support and a variety of fundraising programs are utilized by many dive teams to assure the accessibility of essential equipment.

SCENE EVALUATION

The success of an operation depends directly upon the scene evaluation made by the dive rescue team. Without a detailed assessment prior to entering the water, the dive team may just as well stay home. The quality of the scene evaluation can determine whether an operation is a five-minute task successfully completed, or a five-day exercise in futility.

Enroute to the Scene

Scene evaluation begins the minute the call for help is received. While enroute, the Dive Rescue Specialist gathers such basic information as the nature of the call, water conditions, and (depending upon the team's structure and call out procedure) the dispatcher's success in contacting other dive team members.

Formulating a mental file, dive team members note some obvious, but often overlooked, details. What are the weather conditions? Is a storm in the making? How many hours of remaining daylight? Will other agencies be needed? Should a tow truck be called? Will there be a need for manpower in addition to dive team members? How far from shore did the accident occur? Will the

search be conducted from shore or out of a boat?

Thus, even before arriving at the scene, the Dive Rescue Specialist is thinking of strategy. Of course, upon arrival the situation could be totally different from what was perceived while enroute.

The competent dive team member must keep his mind open to assimilate new information quickly and be prepared to make split-second decisions and changes. Don't develop tunnel vision which is common in pressure situations.

Upon arriving at the scene, the rescue diver's involvement will depend upon whether or not a team leader is present. If the team leader is present he may assign the diver to interview witnesses, change into scuba gear and stand by ready to dive, serve as a liaison with the media, etc.

If a team leader is not yet present, the Dive Rescue Specialist should start gathering information (i.e. nature of accident, number of victims, ages, names, etc). Initiating the scene evaluation will save time and thus allow a more expedient deployment of the dive team when additional members arrive at the scene.

Rescue Mode, Recovery Mode and the Risk/Benefit Factor

Dive team operations should be planned and executed around three terms that will often be referred to in this text: Rescue Mode, Recovery Mode, and the Risk/Benefit Factor. If a dive team does not know whether it is operating in Rescue or Recovery Mode, or what type of Risk/Benefit Factor they are facing, then problems and confusion, with sometimes tragic consequences, are the inevitable result.

Rescue Mode

A Rescue Mode operation is run when there is a chance to save a human life. In Rescue Mode, the Dive Rescue Specialist must make quick decisions, conduct brief witness interviews, and initiate the running of search patterns as other dive team members pursue additional information from witnesses.

A dive team that has done its homework through training and preparation, will be able to respond and operate expeditiously without sacrificing caution. Practice, training and proper equipment ensure effectiveness even when manpower is limited.

Recovery Mode

A Recovery Mode operation is run without the goal of saving a life. For example, when a victim has been underwater for over one hour, or the object of the operation does not involve victims in the water, then the operation is conducted in Recovery Mode.

In Recovery Mode, the operation is executed at a slower, deliberate pace. Witnesses are interviewed in more detail, and more time is taken for documentation and the collection of evidence at the scene. Often,

the Dive Rescue Specialist may determine through the scene evaluation that hazardous conditions such as depth, current or weather, diminish the reasons for diving at all.

Sometimes an operation initiated in Rescue Mode will have to shift into Recovery Mode. This transition should be made subtly — undetectable to the victim's family, friends and onlookers. Simple hand signals, like a tap on a watch, could be used to communicate the team leader's decision to shift to Recovery Mode.

The Risk/Benefit Factor

The Risk/Benefit Factor is a subjective evaluation of the merits of an operation: Does the ultimate payoff (benefit) merit the risks the dive team must take to achieve it? Every operation MUST be assigned a Risk/-Benefit Factor.

This factor is not a numerical figure arrived at through complex calculations. It is much simpler than that, yet ironically it is often overlooked. Ignoring it has proven fatal to dive team members.

When there is a chance to save a life — a Rescue Mode operation — then the potential benefit will be considered high. The dive team responding in Rescue Mode, with a potentially high benefit, will be able to justify a certain amount of risk.

This is not to say that reckless moves or sloppy decisions are justified in such cases, any more than an ambulance driver enroute to the hospital is justified in driving recklessly.

It is suprising how many dive teams take high risks for relatively low benefits. By the authors' calculations, approximately 90 percent of the nation's dive team fatalities occur during operations executed in Recovery Mode — operations where there was no chance to save a victim's life in the first place.

As we detail the procedures for dive team training, equipment, and the execution of a variety of operations, we will often refer to the Rescue and Recovery Mode responses and the Risk/Benefit Factors involved.

The Last-Seen-Point

The dive team has a primary objective when responding to a dive call — the establishment of the "last-seen-point." The last seen point eliminates a great deal of uncertainty from an underwater search. This is true whether the operation is in Rescue or Recovery Mode.

Many times the dive team may have to work with more than one last-seen-point. Often the estimated last seen points of witnesses will be close together. However, all information should be recorded and considered according to its own merits.

Without a last-seen-point, reasons to even enter the water are rare, unless other evidence can be found near the shore or in the water to support a possible last-seen-point.

The most common use of the last-seen-point is the location of a drowning victim. Two pertinent facts enhance the value of the last-seen-point. The first is that a drowning victim will invariably sink right to the bottom without stopping — including drowning situations in moving water such as rivers and canals.

The second is that the victim is often found on the bottom contour within a radius from the last-seen-point which is equal to the depth of the water. For example, if the victim were to drown in 30 feet of water, the body is likely to be found on the bottom within a 30 foot radius from the point on the bottom contour directly below the last-seen-point topside.

There are three basic components to establishing the last-seen-point:
1) Witness Interviews.
2) Use of Reference Points and Reference Objects.
3) Physical Evidence.

Interviewing Witnesses

Obtaining information from witnesses is a skill which is best gained through years of experience. Many dive team members have acquired this experience through their primary professions as police officers or firefighters.

Dive team members, such as civilian volunteers, who have not had significant experience in witness interviewing, would be wise to solicit training in this aspect. Often, a local law enforcement agency will oblige the volunteer force with an informative workshop on the subject.

The manner in which witness interviewing is approached can make the difference between minutes and hours when it is time to conduct the underwater search. The Dive Rescue Specialist must consider every available witness as a potential resource, while maintaining control and an objective attitude of the situation.

When the dive team arrives on the scene, witnesses will usually run up to the official vehicle. Inevitably, emotions will run high, there will be chaos and confusion, and a number of fingers will be pointing towards the water. The dive team must take control of the crucial witness interviews, lest valuable time be spent searching the wrong areas.

Witness interviewing is a critical skill. There will be times when compassion must be carefully balanced with firm authority. In some cases, critical information must be obtained from someone in distress, such as the relative of a drowning victim.

Family Members as Witnesses

Family members are naturally going to be under a great deal of stress and must be treated with respect. The best approach is to keep the family contained in one area and inform them of what the dive team's objectives are.

Often, family members themselves are unaware of the lifesaving potential of a dive team even after a victim has been submerged for a certain amount of time. Without making promises, a representative of the dive team should be able to communicate the purpose of the Rescue Mode operation and attempt to derive the best account possible from the family members' statements. The handling of family members will be discussed in greater detail in Chapter Four.

Bystander Witnesses

Bystanders may also experience intense emotions at the scene. Many times a bystander will be consumed with guilt at having witnessed a drowning, for example, without being able to do more to help the victim. As with the family, the dive team must be compassionate towards bystanders while maintaining firm control and carefully evaluating their statements.

Child Witnesses

Children are often viewed as unreliable witnesses, however, they do see the same things that adults see and often their testimony is not tainted with strong emotions nor an awareness of the grim nature of the accident. Young witnesses often will respond more favorably to a female interviewer.

Questionable Witnesses

At times the emotions at a drowning scene will combine with the temperament of certain witnesses to create difficulties for the dive team. The testimony of intoxicated or emotionally unbalanced witnesses should not be ruled out automatically (they may be the only witnesses available at times). But the dive team should consider cautiously the reliability of witnesses who may be under the influence of alcohol or drugs.

Similarly, a disoriented survivor of a boat or vehicle accident may mislead the dive team to search for a nonexistent victim. Conversely, the disoriented survivor may lead first responders to believe there are no other victims when in fact there are.

Such situations are particularly difficult because any surviving victim can understandably be traumatized. However, the dive team member should be aware that such false information is possible. No matter what the survivors may say, the dive team will have to cover the scene thoroughly to assure themselves that there are no additional victims.

Separating Witnesses

When interviewing witnesses, separate them from one another to obtain individual accounts of the accident. You want to avoid a composite impression from a variety of sources. It would be much better to have two separate areas to search, than one search area which resulted from the collaboration of two witnesses, both of whom are compromising their individual observations.

Separately interviewed witnesses often have better recall than when they are interviewed in the presence of others — particularly when they are with a dominating personality who may influence their statements.

On The Scene

Witness Collaboration

A good example of the distortion caused by collaboration among witnesses occurred at a drowning in a large reservoir. There were five witnesses — four young men and a young woman. The young men, fraternity brothers who had been drinking all afternoon, were loud and overbearing when the dive team arrived on the scene.

During questioning by dive team members, they appeared much more confident of their observations than did the woman, who was not one of their group. She pointed out a different location than the fraternity brothers did, and timidly stayed in the background.

The dive team focused their efforts on the location where the majority of witnesses (the fraternity brothers) said they saw the victim go down. The initial search was unsuccessful. Several days later, the body refloated at the spot that the female witness had originally pointed out. The dive team was still searching the location designated by the fra-ternity brothers when the body refloated.

In this case, the dive team's error was in not taking into account the collaboration among the fraternity brothers of their eyewitness "recollections" of the incident. The dive team also neglected to consider the impact that drinking had had on the male witnesses.

The fraternity brothers did not intend to mislead the search — they simply did not want to contradict each other. Thus, they inadvertently adjusted their observations, opinions and statements to the satisfaction of each other. In effect, they comprised a single witness — a poor one in light of their intoxication and tendency to collaborate.

The young woman, on the other hand, had lined up a spot where she had last seen the swimmer between the point where she stood during the drowning and a tree on the opposite shore. Her information should have been weighed as much as, if not more than, that of the four fraternity brothers.

Interviewers in Uniform

Some subjects are more receptive to an interviewer in uniform, while others are not. A uniformed officer or dive team member may have greater success with an unruly or intoxicated witness than an interviewer in plainclothes. Often, the strong, informative, father-type of image earns respect.

Women and children will often be more receptive to a female dive team member, or a dive team member not in uniform. Every situation is different and an experienced eye for evaluating witnesses is the greatest help in assessing the best approach.

Using a Reference Object

When asking a witness to point to the last-seen-point, the first step is to take the witness to the exact location where he or she was at the time of the accident.

If witnesses were on shore, then have them stand in the same spot when they saw the incident. If the witnesses were in a boat at the time of the accident, then they should be placed in a boat and brought back to the same location in the water.

Don't rely on distance estimates by witnesses in terms of feet, yards or miles. Give the witness a reference object that he or she can direct to the location where the victim, boat or object was last seen.

The reference object should be as close in size and shape as possible to the object of the search. If you want the witness to point out the last seen point for a swimmer, then put the first diver dressed in the water and have him make a surface swim to the area under the witness's directions.

The first diver dressed can be used as a reference object and establish a last-seen-point by following witness' directions.

If the operation involves a sunken boat, place a boat in the water so the witnesses can relate what they are now seeing as accurately as possible to what they can recollect.

The whole intent of the reference object and this form of questioning is to reenact the accident, thus enhancing the accuracy of the witness's recall. This is necessary even if the accident occurred just minutes before the interview.

The Dive Rescue Specialist will want to avoid having a witness estimate distances in terms of yards, or give such qualitative measurements as "the length of a football field." For one thing, few agree on how far a certain distance is in yards or feet by eyesight, particularly over water.

Interviewers should be careful not to ask such leading questions as: "Is that where you last saw the swimmer?" Instead, ask the witness, "Okay, now tell me, does my swimmer have to go right or left? Farther out or closer in?"

This manner of questioning puts the burden of recall on the witness. Otherwise the witness may unconsciously alter his or her memory to fit the location where the reference object is originally placed in the water.

Professional dive teams that have been using the reference object method over the last several years have often been impressed with the accuracy of witness recall.

The dive team will establish the last-seen-point with a reference object by the following steps:

1) Team leader assigns dive team members to individual witnesses. If there are many witnesses and the operation is in Rescue Mode, then the dive team may want to concentrate initially on key witnesses that are able to communicate quickly and effectively (additional witnesses may be interviewed should the search be prolonged).

2) The interviewer takes the witness back to the exact location where he or she was at the time of the accident.

3) A reference object, similar to the shape and size of object of the search, is placed in the water.

4) The interviewer asks the witness to direct the object (i.e. boat or swimmer) to the last-seen-point.

Don't Confuse Me With The Facts

The effectiveness of developing a last-seen-point, and the futility of not using one, was demonstrated when a motorboat sank in a lake near a residential neighborhood. The boaters swam to shore and the local fire department was called to the scene. A few of the firefighters happened to be divers and brought along their scuba gear.

The divers acknowledged the general area which was pointed out, cleared the beach of all witnesses, and went diving. They searched unsuccessfully for five days.

Finally, the boat's owner requested help from a second dive team. This team arrived in the morning, knocked on the doors of houses around the lake and found a number of eyewitnesses. Utilizing the Reference Object approach, the second dive team had the witnesses help establish the last-seen-point by directing a boat on the water.

Once they had their last-seen-point to work with, the second dive team put a diver in the water and the boat was found on the third sweep of a search pattern. The dive team refloated the boat, towed it back to shore and was home that same day in time for lunch.

The difference in the approaches of the two dive teams was that the first divers were relying strictly upon luck rather than using a strategy such as that employed by the second team. With a good last-seen-point, developed with the use of a reference object, the second team had invested a minimum of underwater time.

Lack of Witnesses

When no eyewitnesses are available, physical evidence can sometimes give clues to the victim's location. Such indicators as damage to manmade structures or natural objects (i.e. bridges or trees in the event of a vehicle-in-the-water accident), or traces of victim activity on shore (footprints, clothing) can contribute to finding a good search area.

An example of physical evidence in lieu of witness testimony helping to establish a search area occurred in the drowning of two duckhunters. Their capsized boat and several decoys were found floating near the lake shore.

Rather than search the area where the boat was found, the dive team took a compass reading and went to the opposite side of the lake. The divers hypothesized that the duck hunters would have been on the other shore, in the reeds, rather than trying to hunt from the exposed shore — the wind had probably drifted the boat and decoys to the other side. The underwater search proved their hypothesis correct and yielded the bodies shortly after the first diver went down.

One body recovery operation was completed with the help of the victim's dog. The young man had gone cliff diving with just his dog as a companion. Not realizing the shallowness of the water, the cliff diver broke his neck and sank to the bottom. The victim was missing for several days before friends discovered the dog wandering about unattended.

Finally, the victim's car was located near the cliffs. When the dog was returned to the scene, it went to the water's edge and gazed directly at the spot below which the victim was found by the divers shortly thereafter.

Without eyewitnesses, the dive team may find clues through information about the victim's habits, i.e. the solitary fisherman, swimmer, cliff diver, etc. In short, the lack of an eyewitness does not completely cancel out the chances for a successful recovery operation.

When there are no eyewitnesses, be cautious not to let others do your scene evaluation for you. Valuable time and dive team resources can be wasted following the hunches of bystanders.

One sheriff, for example, had a theory that a victim's body will react in water in the same manner as a 100-pound sack of potatoes. When a victim drowned in a river, the sheriff tossed in the full potato sack while the dive team was enroute. When the team arrived the sheriff sent them to a spot a half-mile away. However, the victim was found less than 20 feet from where he went under the water.

The Scene Sketch

Do not rely on memory when compiling information from witnesses. A notepad is an essential piece of equipment for compiling

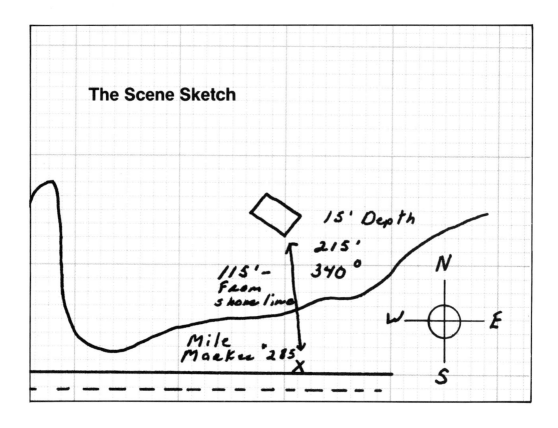

The Scene Sketch

the scene sketch and all pertinent data collected during the operation.

A simple notepad, with blank sheets of paper, is better than a standard accident form for the initial compilation and sketch — accident forms tend to be cumbersome and can bog the Dive Rescue Specialist down with unnecessary details during the actual operation.

Naturally, such forms will have to be completed, but that can be done later without inhibiting progress. Some dive teams, however, use a form specifically for on-scene documentation. These forms work very well by preventing oversights.

The initial scene sketch does not have to be elaborate, but it must detail the last-seen-points, significant landmarks, measurements and angles, and areas being covered by search patterns. After the operation is completed, the scene sketch should be done in detail.

Accuracy and attention to detail are important as scene sketches often play important roles, such as serving as evidence in court.

Witness Follow-Up

Before any witnesses leave the scene, make certain they have given complete information on where they can be contacted. On a long, drawn-out operation, the witnesses may have to be called back to the scene and reinterviewed.

Ask the witnesses to produce legal I.D.s, do not take their word for their identification. One reason for this is that there have been times when a curious suspect will return to a crime scene to watch the subsequent diving operation.

Careful questioning with the use of reference objects and a clear scene sketch minimize the necessity for reinterviewing witnesses, but calling witnesses back is an option that must always be preserved.

Normally, a non-team member, such as a law enforcement officer, will be on hand to get the details (names, phone numbers, addresses, etc.) from witnesses. However, the Dive Rescue Specialist must always be prepared to make provisions for witness follow-up himself.

On The Scene

The Witnesses Went Home?

The following lake drowning serves as an example of the importance of being able to access witnesses later: Four youths at a church picnic had an impromptu swimming race. When they got to the other side, there were only three of them. Nobody actually saw the victim go under.

The sheriff's department was called, the witnesses were interviewed briefly,

and the search initiated as the witnesses were sent home. The following day, the dive team was called and requested to talk to the witnesses at the scene.

The witnesses were returned and the exact route of the boys' swimming race was determined. With this information, the dive team was able to find the victim's body within an hour.

The Flying Reference Object

One of the most dramatic examples of the effectiveness of the last-seen-point, reference object, scene sketch and witness follow-up was the recovery of a plane from a Canadian reservoir.

More than a decade had passed since the single engine plane sank during an attempted water take-off in the Ghost Lake Reservoir near Calgary, Alberta. The pilot and two passengers drowned and their bodies refloated days after the accident. The plane, however, mysteriously disappeared without yielding a trace of physical evidence.

Numerous amateur and professional dive teams conducted a variety of search operations for the next ten years. Finding the aircraft had become somewhat of an obsession for the various parties of divers hoping to gain fame for the discovery.

Over $150,000 was spent by the various search parties who employed a wide array of sophisticated apparatus. But all these efforts produced no clues, let alone the plane.

Finally, the Calgary Fire Department Dive Team undertook the search for the lost plane by reinterviewing witnesses and establishing a solid last-seen-point. For a reference object, the Calgary divers constructed a makeshift "plane" out of boards and sheets mounted on a boat. Witnesses who saw the plane's fateful take-off attempt ten years earlier, directed the reference object to the last-seen-point — the spot where the plane sank.

After several days of topside preparation, the actual diving began. The plane was found within 30 minutes — less than 20 feet from the Calgary dive team's established last-seen-point.

Other First Responders

The dive team can increase its effectiveness by training other first responders (law enforcement, fire department and shore patrol) to obtain the type of information needed for the establishment of a last-seen-point.

Too often, there have been incidents where a responding agency will remove evidence or dismiss witnesses before the dive team arrives. One of the more tactful ways to inform members of other related agencies is to invite them to the dive team's training sessions dealing with scene evaluation. The dive team's relationship with other agencies will be discussed in greater detail later in this text.

Summary

The importance of the scene evaluation cannot be overemphasized. The atmosphere at a water accident scene is nearly always dramatic, sometimes hysterical, and the public safety diver must conduct an effective scene evaluation despite the inevitable outside pressures from family, friends and members of the other agencies.

This rule applies whether the operation is conducted in Rescue Mode or Recovery Mode. The Dive Rescue Specialist must always make a methodical evaluation of the situation at hand. Otherwise, he is relying upon luck rather than strategy.

FAMILY, MEDIA AND OTHER AGENCIES

At the scene of a drowning, the victim's family is experiencing severe emotional trauma. Members of the media are often at the scene trying to get as much information as they can so they can rush back to their offices to file stories under a deadline. Departmental officials, usually law enforcement agents, are on hand and, like the dive team, are feeling pressed to seek a speedy resolution to the situation.

Practically everybody at the scene is under some degree of pressure. It is inevitable that interests of the various parties will conflict despite the mutual goal of retrieving the victim.

In such emotionally-charged situations, the involved personalities can be unpredictable. Often, the family feels the need to do anything other than sit and wait. A rookie reporter may become a nuisance, getting in the way of the operation. A local official unfamiliar with underwater rescue techniques may try to direct your divers' actions.

Therefore, the professional dive team must learn to handle the assortment of personalities with tact and efficiency. Interpersonal relationships must never hamper the objectives of the dive team at the scene.

Keep in mind, however, that the relationship between the dive rescue team and the family, media and other agencies has an effect reaching far beyond the scope of the immediate operation.

Handling the Family

Knowing that their loved one is out there somewhere, underwater and out of sight, creates a strong mixture of grief and frustration for the family. The situation requires compassion, tact and rules of procedure on the part of the dive team. While representatives from other agencies usually are at the scene, it is the dive team that the family looks to for the answers.

Keep the family together. If possible, put them in an official vehicle, where they will feel that they are part of the operation, turn off the radio and keep a team member with them.

This team member should keep the family informed on the progress of the operation. He should do his best to explain what is going on and why. It is important that this person be familiar with the dive team's methods, if not a dive team member himself. When speaking to the family about the victim, always use the victim's first name. This small detail helps the family see that the dive team is taking a personal interest in the operation.

Honesty from the onset is the best policy when dealing with a victim's family. If you don't tell them exactly what is going on from the beginning, they will start to draw their own conclusions.

For example, if team members are reinterviewing witnesses in order to establish a better last-seen-point, the family may wonder why divers are out of the water and talking to people (interviewing witnesses) rather than continuing to dive. Naturally, there will be some information that will have to be tempered with consideration for the shock and adjustments the family is going through.

As detailed in Chapter Three, the operation shifts from Rescue Mode to Recovery Mode after the victim has been underwater for more than an hour. Again, this transition should be made subtly. Likewise, when a victim's body is located, this news is passed on quietly among dive team members, and the family is informed gently and appropriately by the dive team's representative.

Should the family begin to have the slightest doubt in the dive team's actions, they could create problems at the scene and later. In some unfortunate situations, an anguished family's criticism of the dive team will appear in media accounts of the incident — unwarranted criticism which resulted from lack of communication rather than ineffectiveness on the part of the dive team.

Operations Going into the Next Day

Usually it is difficult for the family to understand why the operation usually ceases at night (unless the operation is being conducted in Rescue Mode) or must be called off completely.

The dive team spokesman should explain such factors as depth, temperature, entanglement combined with poor visibility and the problems they can present to the underwater operation. In such instances, the dive team spokesman may explain the Risk/ Benefit Factor to the family.

While they are grieving the loss of their loved one, the family will often agree that it won't help matters to risk another life in the process of trying to recover the body.

Use discretion in each case, but it may be helpful to explain some aspects of the process of body refloat. Inform them that you will ask local authorities to make regular checks of the area for the body should it refloat.

Ideally, when shutting down an operation for the evening, have the area lighted and patrolled. With lights, a portable generator, possibly a team vehicle, and somebody on duty, the family will be assured that the operation is being maintained should they come back to the scene during the night.

Have patrol personnel check the shoreline periodically during the night in case the body should have refloated and drifted to shore. Avoid letting this detail take on the appearance of a weekend camping trip.

Encourage the family to leave the scene before the dive team does and give them a firm time when the operation will commence in the morning. It is important that the dive team arrives at the scene at least an hour earlier than the time you scheduled for the family. In the majority of cases, the family will arrive at the scene earlier than they were told. Avoid having family members pacing around at the scene wondering when the dive team is going to show up.

Upon Locating the Body

When the body is located, this information is passed along silently to the team leader and/or spokesman to the family with a quiet signal.

In keeping with the policy of informing the family, the dive team spokesman should then tell the family that the victim has been found and will be taken to the appropriate location, such as the hospital or morgue.

Normally, the body should be bagged underwater (this procedure will be discussed in a later chapter), but it is still appropriate to remove the family from the scene prior to resurfacing the victim.

An exception to the above procedure is the emotional situation where the behavior of a family member or members foreshadows problems when the body is resurfaced. If you feel the family's cooperation is in question, direct them away from the scene temporarily before resurfacing the body. Sending them to the sheriff's office for additional interviewing is one possiblity. From there the family can be directed to the morgue or hospital.

The dive team has a responsibility to minimize the emotional turmoil at the scene out of consideration not for just the family, but for the divers as well. It is hard enough to dive and recover dead victims, and there is no reason why a diver should have to stand by while a hysterical family, often including small children, mourns over the corpse on shore. Also, when a situation deteriorates to this point, it becomes virtually impossible to control.

At the morgue, attendants will have a few moments to make the body as presentable as possible before letting the family members view it. There is some debate among grief counselors about whether it is best to let the family view the victim at the scene, or wait until going to the morgue. The authors do not wish to argue that point, nor do we feel it is necessary. Experience has shown that viewing the body at the hosptial or morgue is the easier for all parties concerned.

Dealing with the Media

Media relations can be a hindrance or an asset to the dive team. If handled correctly, the local media can be one of the dive team's greatest allies in public relations and fund-raising efforts. Fortunately, the majority of media personnel are cooperative with underwater rescue and recovery teams and often, positive relationships are established between a dive team and the local media.

Members of the media do not need to find fault with diving operations to create interest. A well-executed operation is usually interesting enough to satisfy even the most curious journalist and provide colorful footage or stories.

The best methods for dealing with the media are similar, in some respects, to dealing with family members. Have one person serve as the team spokesman to the media. This spokesman does not necessarily have to be a dive team member, although that would be ideal.

Often a member of the local sheriff's office or another agency related to the operation will be able to serve as the media liaison while the dive team goes about their business undistracted. However, make sure that this spokesman understands dive team protocol and operations.

Such delegation of at-the-scene media relations prevents misunderstandings between dive team members and reporters, and assures the accuracy of information being released to the public. On some operations it is necessary to have one person stay with the media to make sure reporters stay out of the way.

By keeping the media contained within one area and keeping them posted on the progress of the operation, a better result is possible for all involved. The best way to deal with the media is to keep in mind that they are under deadline pressure to produce news not yet known to the general public.

Often there will be details that cannot be appropriately released to the media, such as a victim's name. However, a brief synopsis of the situation could be enough to let them do their reporting job without compromising the dive team operation. For example, if a car rolls into a lake with a five-year-old boy locked inside and the hysterical mother is being interviewed by the dive team while divers search in Rescue Mode, the following account could be released to the media:

"A five-year-old boy is trapped in his family's car underwater. Our divers are searching for the car and will attempt to retrieve the victim. A medivac helicopter is standing by to evacuate the youth upon retrieval. We will not know for sure why the car went into the water until a firsthand investigation is made. There is no evidence of foul play at this time."

In the above example, neither the victim's nor the family's name is released. The mother is not subjected to on-scene interviews and speculations of foul play are quelled from the start. Should this turn out to be a case which merits a criminal investigation, there will be plenty of time to report on that later. In such a case, the media will be interviewing the local law enforcement agent charged with the investigation.

A major problem with media and drowning accidents is the tendency for TV crews and newspaper photographers to seek explicit footage or photos of bodies. The dive team can do several things to discreetly avoid the additional trauma to the family caused by having the victim's body exhibited to the public. Methods for dealing with these situations will be detailed in a later chapter.

Be careful not to alienate the media unnecessarily. An example of the repercussions possible occurred during a body recovery operation in the northwest. A vehicle had plunged into a lake next to a truckstop late at night.

The next morning representatives of the news media were poised on the shore at the spot where the obvious trail of debris had led them. The dive team leader knew that the body recovery operation would be closely monitored by the media. To avoid gruesome photographs, he had a sheriff's boat serve as the body transport, while deputies onshore lured the reporters and photographers to another location. While it served its purpose, the decoy method also infuriated some members of the media.

The evening news that night criticized the dive team for its apparent "lack of organization." The lesson learned from the misunderstanding was, according to that particular dive team leader, do not attempt to deceive the media.

Try to cooperate as much as is within reason with media representatives. In the event that questions cannot be answered appropriately, the team spokesman is within his rights to state that the matter is still under investigation. In particularly awkward situations, a written press release might be necessary to minimize the possibility of misquotes.

Dealing with Other Agencies

To be of maximum service to their community, the dive team must have a well-coordinated relationship with the other local emergency service agencies. The time to establish this working relationship is not at the accident scene, but in the preplanning stages. In other words, these relationships should result from crisis management, not management-by-crisis.

Orient the local law enforcement, fire safety, emergency medical and support services (i.e. tow truck operators) to the dive team's needs and protocol. When they understand the specific problems of underwater

rescue and recovery, these agencies will become indispensable allies of the dive team.

Without understanding and communication between the dive team and these other agencies most operations will become much more complicated than they need be.

For example, if local law enforcement or shore patrol personnel understand the necessity of establishing a good last-seen point, they can be helpful when encountering witnesses prior to the dive team's arrival at the scene. On the other hand, if officials do not understand the last seen point technique, they may send witnesses home, or remove physical evidence without even marking the location.

One of the most awkward situations occurs when a non-team member attempts to direct divers. A team leader will sometimes have to tactfully assert his control and explain the

Dealing with other agencies — Divers work with FAA and NTSB investigators following an air crash into a mountain lake.

team actions and strategy. However, with the team that is well-trained, properly equipped and follows the proper procedures, this situation should seldom arise.

As stated previously, members of other local agencies will be needed for such tasks as crowd control, witness follow-up, night patrol and other facets of the operation. Also, the dive team often will receive its best candidates directly from the ranks of these other agencies.

Law enforcement agents and fire service personnel already have the emergency service background and professional attributes that make many of them ideal dive team members. In addition, resources already in place, such as communications systems or a firehouse in which to base the dive truck for quick response, can greatly enhance a dive team's service to the community.

The dive team that has proven itself in the field will be remembered favorably by the fire chief or sheriff when budget time rolls around. It is the responsibility of the dive team and its members to see that the team proves itself to be worth the time and money that members of other agencies and the community invest in it.

When called to a mutual-aid operation, the requesting agency must understand that the dive team being summoned may have their own protocol. The efforts of the dive team(s) and other agencies should all be coordinated with on-scene officials respecting the authority of the team leader over his divers. A non-diver or member of another agency should not be directing the actions of individual divers. All requests must be made through the dive team leadership and coordinated with the overall diving operation.

In some instances, a dive team leader may have to assert his authority for the safety of an operation. For example, a southern dive team was summoned to help an inexperienced dive team on a recovery operation. Upon arrival, the dive team leader of the requested dive team could see that the original divers were having difficulty with their basic scuba skills. The dive team leader told the relevant authorities that he would not put his divers in the water until the other divers surfaced and stayed topside. Such mandates may at times be necessary for an effective operation.

Normally, a mutual-aid operation is conducted in Recovery Mode. Therefore, there is plenty of time for a thorough briefing of the dive teams and agencies involved. When one or more dive teams are operating together, it is imperative that their efforts are coordinated and that they are using uniform procedures.

Dealing with the Medical Community

A solid relationship between the dive team and the local medical community can pay off in several ways. Today, it has become increasingly important that dive teams pre-arrange the medical treatment of potential victims. Without well-coordinated efforts between dive teams and medical personnel, rescue operations involving cold-water near-drowning are impossible.

An increasing number of medical teams are willing to work to resuscitate near-drowning victims today. However, there are still many areas where doctors and hospital staffs are unaware of their own lifesaving potential through recent medical advances.

The dive team can be instrumental in supplying updated information from medical journals and news reports on the growing number of near-drowning saves.

One of the best ways to establish this relationship is through contact with medical experts who are familiar with the procedures for treating near-drowning victims. Dive teams needing such references should contact the International Association of Dive Rescue Specialists or Dive Rescue Inc./International, (303) 482-0887; 2619 Canton Court, Fort Collins, Colorado 80525.

Cooperation with local medical personnel can result in effective public education programs benefitting the efforts of both the dive team and the medical community.

Summary

Many dive teams are isolated from other local emergency service agencies and the general public until they are needed. A familiarity with local fire, police and paramedic protocols, and a working relationship with the media, will streamline dive team operations.

Relations with the victim's friends and family will always be a sensitive area. The dive team, however, can do much to help alleviate the shock of the tragedy through professional conduct. In seemingly inconsolable circumstances, Dive Rescue Specialists will at least have the assurance that they have done their best.

The dive team that performs well in the field will be rewarded with favorable publicity, cooperation from local authorities, and, in many cases, funding support. Thus the human factors involved will affect the dive team both in and out of the field.

SEARCH PATTERNS

A dive team's skill, or lack of skill, becomes evident when it is time to run the search pattern. A given area underwater can only be effectively searched by a dive team that thoroughly understands the intent and proper execution of effective search techniques (via search patterns).

The search pattern is the heart of most underwater rescue and recovery operations. More often than not it is virtually impossible to find an object underwater, even something as large as a car or a boat, without an established method of search. There are a variety of good search patterns and methods. Some involve one diver, two divers on a buddy system, tow sleds or the use of compasses. However, as with the entire operational plan, the simplest method is usually the most effective.

An effective search pattern must have the following attributes:

1) The search pattern starts at a known point, covers a known area, and ends at a known point — which results in either finding the object of the search, or confirming that the object is not in that specific area.

2) Allows for clear communication between the diver and surface personnel through line signals or communication system for direction or calls for assistance.

3) Is adaptable to various environments such as zero visibility or under the ice.

4) Should not require sophisticated nor expensive equipment — can be run with basic scuba gear.

5) Provides the ability to mark the location of found objects.

6) Can be adapted to finding objects of various size such as those ranging from a handgun to a vehicle.

7) Is simple enough that the dynamics of the pattern can be explained to a helpful bystander/line tender during an emergency situation.

8) Does not require great amounts of manpower, but can utilize available divers effectively by running numerous patterns simultaneously.

9) Can be run from shore or out of a boat.

10) Allows for buddy team diving, or one diver down with a safety diver topside ready to respond to signal for assistance.

Search Pattern

Line

The major tool of a search pattern is the line. Professional dive teams have found that 1/4 inch, braided polypropylene line to be the most suitable line for the job. Polypropylene increases the line's buoyancy and is much easier to handle underwater than heavier lines such as hemp rope which tend to absorb water. Also, the smaller diameter rope creates less drag in the water. A dive team should stock at least 600 feet of the line in 200 foot lengths.

Stuff Bags

The polypropylene line does have a tendency to twist and kink in a manner that could eventually make it unmanageable. Thus, the solution is to store the line in "stuff bags." Manufactured out of screen mesh, stuff bags enable the user to wash and dry the line while it is stored. The line is fed into the bag through a narrow opening in the top.

Stuff bags also enable the user to deploy line quickly while containing excess line, thus minimizing the confusion of excess line at the scene.

Note: When stuffing the line into the bag, make sure to do it only a few inches at a time. If bunches of the line are wadded up and put in the bag it will not deploy properly.

Line Tender Equipment

Every line tender must have a watch, compass, notepad and a personal flotation device (PFD) or a lifevest. He or she will be monitoring the down time and PSI of the diver(s) on the other end of the line, and must not depend upon spot checks with bystanders and other team members for this critical information.

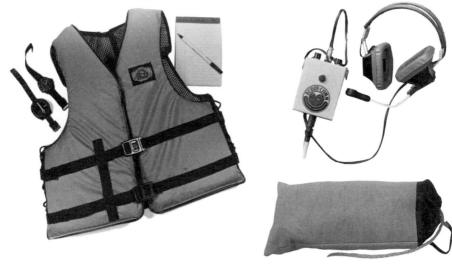

Stuff bags enable rapid line deployment as well as provide storage. Hardwire communications systems, like BUDDY-COMM, contribute to diver's safety and efficiency. Watch, compass, PFD and notepad are standard gear for line tenders.

Equipment

The line tender must be constantly aware of the diver's movements and needs immediate access to one standard timepiece. The compass, as mentioned earlier, is used to take a reading to develop last-seen-points and also in the development of search pattern areas or boundaries. These readings, along with other pertinent information (i.e. diver's PSI throughout the operation), are recorded in the line tender's notepad.

It is important that each line tender has his or her own equipment. The line tender should avoid sharing or misplacing essential equipment needed to insure the safety of the diver at the other end of the line.

Marker Buoys

There are two types of marker buoys: Submersible buoys are neutrally buoyant until deployed from underwater and can be used for marking the victim's body and other objects found underwater. Surface buoys are used to mark the boundaries of a water accident, searched areas, and the last seen point. When using marker buoys, however, there is the extra hazard of more line(s) in the water.

Again, the Risk/Benefit Factor determines whether or not the benefit of marker buoys is worth the added risk of entanglement or confusion created by additional line. Also, in Rescue Mode, the time spent placing marker buoys could be valuable time better spent searching.

Search Pattern Weight

While searching deep water or outside the limits of a shore-based pattern, a boat-based search pattern (line tender in boat or in scuba gear and below boat underwater) is used. Sometimes it is necessary to anchor not only the boat, but also a pivotal point of the pattern if the angle of the line between the tender and the diver is too steep to run a smooth pattern.

The search pattern weight allows for the adjustment of the searchline which runs parallel to the anchor line, through a carabiner or pulley attached to the weight on the bottom contour, and out to the diver.

The diver is now able to search an area in the same manner as he would from shore except instead of the pivot point being on shore it is now directly off the search pattern weight on the bottom contour. While a weight can be designed specifically for this purpose, a variety of inexpensive, heavy objects, such as tractor tire rims, often work just as well.

Additional Search Pattern Equipment

Depending upon the most common calls in their respective communities, and the resources available, there is a wide range of sophisticated detection and communications equipment available. However, advanced equipment will require advanced training for such equipment to be effective. For 95 percent of most dive team operations, the basic techniques and equipment detailed in this chapter will suffice.

Most Effectively Used Search Patterns

Keeping in mind the need for simplicity, control by the line tender, and the variety of conditions for each particular search (i.e. depth, bottom contour, visibility), the dive team should be able to apply one of the following search patterns to the majority of operations.

When a search pattern has been completed in an area, there should be no doubt that the area has been covered. If the object was not found, then the dive team must be able to conclude with some degree of certainty that the object is not in that area. Otherwise, the time and effort put into running the search pattern was wasted. As mentioned at the beginning of this chapter, the search pattern selected must be able to give the dive team the satisfaction that they have covered every inch of that particular area.

Surface-Controlled Search Patterns

The most practical arrangement of search patterns involve a working relationship between the diver(s) and a line tender.

As the line tender monitors the progress of the search while controlling one end of the line, the diver swims in the directions predesignated by the pattern selected — thus the tender and diver become a team covering a given area as they simultaneously fill their respective roles topside and underwater.

The line tender is always aware of the location of the last-seen-point and is in constant contact with other topside personnel. The line tender can call the diver back to the surface or change the diver's location on a moment's notice.

Line Signals

Line tenders, primary divers, safety divers and all other dive team members should be thoroughly trained in the use of line signals and briefly review the signals before every operation.

It should be noted that there are many different types of line signals. The U.S. Navy, for example, has a complex system of signals which work well for their operations. The dive rescue team, however, should keep their signals as simple and straightforward as possible. Unless one uses the signals constantly, it is easy to become confused with complex signals.

Following are the basic signals used by many dive teams around the country:

Line Tender to Diver
    two tugs — stop, change direction and take out line
    three tugs — come to surface
Diver to Tender
    two tugs — need more line
    three tugs — have found object of search
    four plus tugs — need help

One tug is not usually used as a line signal as it would be too easy to misinterpret a snag or an unintentional pull as a signal. In cases where it is used, however, it can serve as an affirmative signal (i.e. the line tender's one tug means, "Is everything all right?" and the diver's one tug response means, "Affirmative."

A word of caution: Many dive teams are going to hardwire communications systems. While these systems are an excellent benefit to an operation's safety and efficiency, it is still important that line signals be reviewed and used if necessary as a backup in case of failure of that communications system.

The Sweep Search Pattern

This pattern can be used in a majority of dive team operations. Normally, the sweep search pattern is run from shore, a bridge, a dam or a pier. However, it also can be applied during a boat-based operation under the right conditions. Under ideal conditions, a pattern can be run up to 200 feet from the line tender.

During the execution of the pattern, the diver swims back and forth in arcs which are controlled by the tender. All the time there is tension in the line and constant communication between tender and diver through line signals.

The diver's starting point will depend upon the location of the last-seen-point cited by witnesses. For example, in a standard shore-based pattern, the diver is working his way out towards the last-seen-point. Most witnesses will estimate that an accident occurred farther out than it actually did. Thus, the search should begin closer towards shore.

If the last-seen-point is only 50 feet from shore, then the diver could start the pattern half-way from shore and the last-seen-point and quickly cover the area. But if the last-seen-point is 150 feet from shore, the diver will have to begin diving further out (i.e. 100-120 feet from shore) to make good use of his bottom time.

As the diver works his way out, the line tender will let him make wider arcs. The farther from shore a last-seen-point, the greater the chance for witness miscalculations, which the wider arcs can compensate for.

The line tender will usually line the ends of the arcs up with some type of landmark on the opposite shore. In searches involving a large lake or the ocean, the line tender may have to use compass readings to set the parameters of the arcs.

On some searches, a bottom contour tapers sharply to the shoreline, such as at a beach. In such cases, the line tender should avoid running the diver all the way up to shore to prevent persistent sinus and ear equalization problems in the diver.

When a deep drop off is being searched, the divers should swim the deep portion first. Thus, they will conserve energy and

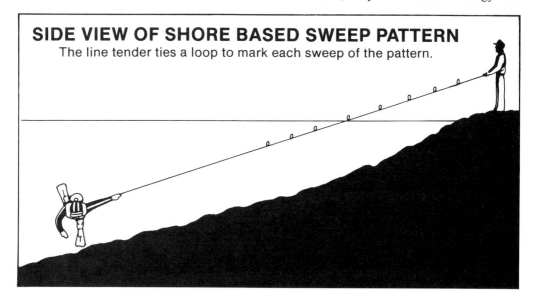

SIDE VIEW OF SHORE BASED SWEEP PATTERN
The line tender ties a loop to mark each sweep of the pattern.

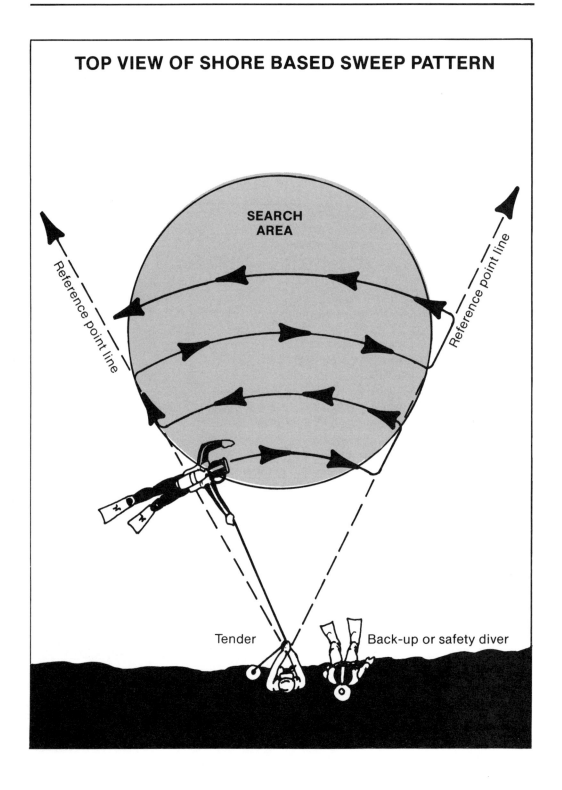

TOP VIEW OF SHORE BASED SWEEP PATTERN

bottom time for the shallower areas, should the search continue.

If there is a large obstruction, such as a boulder underwater, the sweep search pattern can be run to the rock and around the edges. A separate sweep search pattern can be run on the other side later or simultaneously by another line tender/diver pair.

In some cases, a steep drop-off or an underwater cliff can snag a line, thus preventing a consistent sweep by the diver. The dive team has several options in such cases: The line tender can be elevated on shore (which increases the angle of the line); floats can be attached to the line; or the line tender can be placed in a boat (which can be located on the other side of the search area if necessary).

While the sweep pattern is relatively straightforward, flexibility is the key to dealing with factors such as those cited above.

The Parallel Pattern

When searching a large and relatively clean area (free of obstructions), the parallel pattern may be employed. This is particularly advantageous when the object of the search is suspected to be close to shore, but there is a poor last-seen-point.

The line tender and the diver execute this pattern by moving parallel to each other with the tender walking and the diver swimming from a beginning to ending point. At the completion of each pass, the tender will feed the diver more line, both will reverse directions and proceed in the opposite direction.

This pattern works very well off the face of a dam.

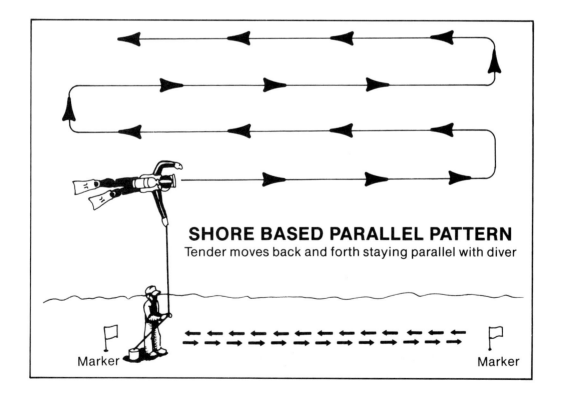

SHORE BASED PARALLEL PATTERN
Tender moves back and forth staying parallel with diver

Marker   Marker

The Snag Method

The snag method can be employed with either a sweep or a parallel pattern. When a large object (i.e. a car) is being sought, and a large area is being searched, a substantial distance can be covered with each pass. The line tender allows the diver more slack than he would during a standard search (where the diver personally covers every inch of the search area). When the object is snagged by the line, the diver then swims to it.

Boat-Based Search Patterns

Many times a water accident occurs farther from shore than a shore-based search pattern can reach. During boat-based search patterns in shallow water, the line tender based in the boat controls the diver's actions while watching his bubbles just as during a sweep pattern from shore.

In deeper water, the boat-based pattern may require the searchline be fed through a carabiner attached to a heavy anchor, which serves as a search pattern weight (see illustration). When using this method, the tender can let the diver complete a 360 degree pass, stop him, and reverse his direction.

This reversal of direction avoids wrapping the search line around the anchor line, and gives the diver a better sense of progress than would swimming in concentric circles. When turning the diver, tender uses either a reference point on shore, such as a tree, or a compass heading.

In the event that the search is being made in shallow water (15 feet or less), it may be

**SHORE BASED
SNAG SEARCH**

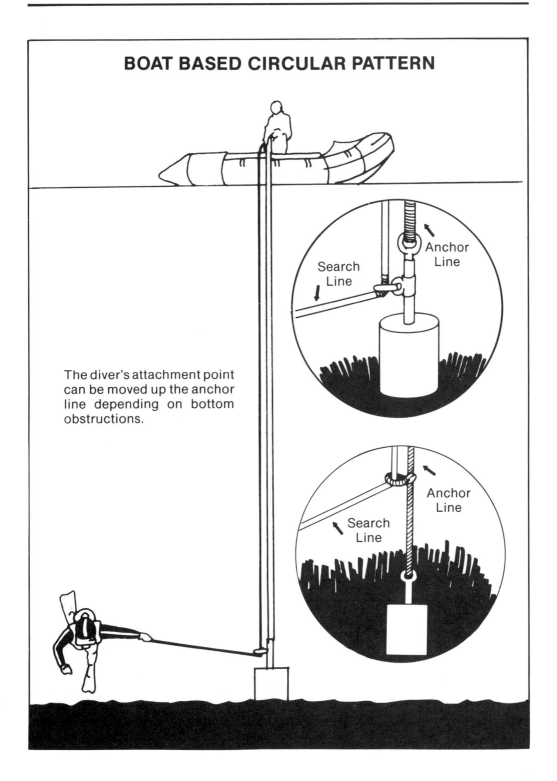

BOAT BASED CIRCULAR PATTERN

Anchor Line

Search Line

The diver's attachment point can be moved up the anchor line depending on bottom obstructions.

Anchor Line

Search Line

more efficient to run a sweep pattern from a boat anchored at least 30 to 40 feet from the last-seen-point.

When water is too rough for the tender to observe the diver's bubbles from topside, it may be possible to put another diver in the water to act as the line tender on the bottom at the search pattern weight (anchor). If another diver is not available, the diver running the pattern may use a weighted line laid out in the search area. When the diver comes to the line he then reverses direction.

Conditions Determining the Search Pattern Used

Visibility
Underwater visibility is one of the major considerations when formulating an operational plan. As mentioned earlier, the diver's visibility may affect the amount of overlap in a search pattern. In zero visibility, the diver often must conduct the entire search by feeling around with his free hand. In shallow areas, divers and other rescue personnel should avoid wading or treading water as stirring up sediment will greatly reduce visibility.

Also, wading can actually destroy evidence that otherwise could have been observed and recovered with minimal damage through search patterns carefully executed by divers. In one case, law enforcement officials waded a shallow section of river before calling in the dive team. When the dive team initiated their search, they discovered the missing evidence — ground into the bottom contour by the waders' footsteps.

Depth
Depth is another factor that can determine the type of search pattern best for an operation. Also, as mentioned previously, depth can limit or cancel an operation completely, depending upon the divers' experience and the Risk/Benefit Factor assigned the operation.

Searching deep waters can require an excessive amount of line and create an awkward angle inhibiting the diver's progress. These situations often require the pattern be run off a search pattern weight as detailed earlier in boat-based patterns, or one of the versions detailed for shore-based patterns for deep water. Depth will also reduce,

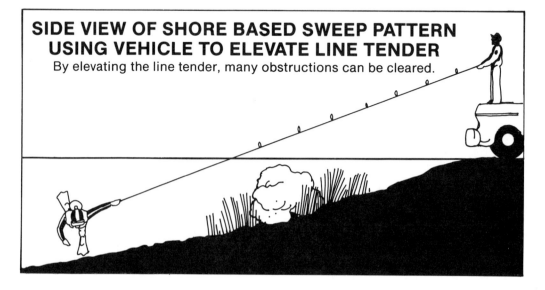

SIDE VIEW OF SHORE BASED SWEEP PATTERN USING VEHICLE TO ELEVATE LINE TENDER
By elevating the line tender, many obstructions can be cleared.

sometimes drastically, the diver's bottom time while running the pattern.

Bottom Contour

The diver's task is much easier when there is a smooth bottom contour. When the bottom is littered with debris, large rocks and other obstructions, the line tender on shore may need to elevate himself somehow, such as by standing in a pickup truck bed, to increase the angle of the line from the diver to the tender. However, this technique is usually only advantageous when the object searched for is close to shore.

Also, weeds and obstructions can be cleared by attaching one or two buoys, as mentioned earlier, to a point in the search-line between the tender and the diver.

In some cases a large obstruction might

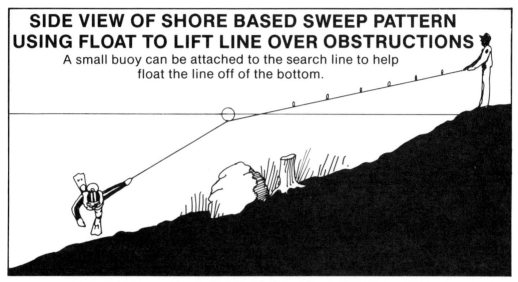

SIDE VIEW OF SHORE BASED SWEEP PATTERN USING FLOAT TO LIFT LINE OVER OBSTRUCTIONS

A small buoy can be attached to the search line to help float the line off of the bottom.

SIDE VIEW OF SHORE BASED SWEEP PATTERN USING SECOND DIVER TO CLEAR OBSTRUCTIONS

A second diver can act as a secondary line tender to help clear obstructions.

actually serve as a search pattern boundary. Some obstructions on the bottom may require a line tender in scuba gear standing on the bottom himself to create the pivot point in the search pattern line and to relay signals from the surface tender.

Number of Divers

In Rescue Mode, the dive team leader may want every suited up diver in the water searching different areas with their individual line tenders. However, there should always be the option of calling one of the divers quickly to the surface to be redirected to the aid of another diver. In Recovery Mode, where the pace is slower, a backup diver should always be standing by to respond to a help signal as emphasized in the previous chapter.

Simplicity is usually the best approach when selecting a search pattern. Don't put a diver in the water just for the sake of on-lookers at the scene. The single diver is usually more efficient than two divers while running most search patterns. Again, the Risk/Benefit Factor is the major consideration whether operating in either Rescue Mode or Recovery Mode.

The Line Tender

The line tender's responsibilities begin with the dressing of the diver. During this phase of the operation, the line tender makes sure the diver is properly dressed and equipped while at the same time a predive checklist is reviewed.

During the actual execution of the search pattern, it is the line tender who serves as the controlling factor of the operation. There are search patterns where the line tender is another diver underwater, but usually it is best that the line tender be topside, based either on shore or in a boat. In this way, the entire operation can be viewed clearly in relation to the last-seen-point and topside

landmarks or compass headings.

The actions of the line tender are similar to that of a fisherman. The line tender keeps a controlling tension on the line, is the sole communicator with the diver, and directs the diver's efforts through a series of line signals.

It is important for the line tender to remain in a fixed position while the diver is running the pattern. The tender must stay in place as if he or she were glued to the ground. Many line tenders will drive a small stake in the ground next to their feet to insure this stability.

Naturally, this fixed position will be much harder to maintain while based in a boat. However, in all types of situations the line tender should be aware that a movement as seemingly insignificant as changing arm position could make a big difference to the diver underwater — sometimes to the point of disorienting the diver.

In Rescue Mode, the line tender may receive information that indicates a better search area while the diver is running a pattern underwater. In such cases, the skilled line tender can change the location of the diver, thus the area the search pattern covers, without resurfacing the diver. To do this, the tender walks toward the new location as the diver is swimming in that direction. Such skills and techniques have made it possible to rescue drowning victims within a few minutes of the dive team's arrival at the scene.

The line tender is also responsible for tracking and documenting the diver's PSI. Even in situations where visibility is good enough that a diver can easily read his gauges, the line tender should summon the diver to the surface periodically and ask for a PSI reading. The line tender also monitors the diver's down time, keeping in mind that the diver should have at least 500 lbs. of air when he surfaces. He or she also monitors the diver's bottom time making sure it stays within the parameters of the decompression tables.

The line tender can develop the ability to gauge the diver's PSI by comparing the reduction of PSI with time increments at which he requests the diver's PSI. The line tender should be able to develop the skill to estimate his diver's PSI within 200 pounds at all times during the dive. Note: Different divers will consume their air at different rates. Because of the critical nature of this task, the line tender should be a trained and experienced member of the dive team.

The line tender assists the diver while dressing. Should the diver overlook an item, such as a knife, the line tender should automatically strap the knife to the diver. A good

---

Search Pattern Pre-Dive Checklist

When formulating the operational plan, the line tender and the divers must run through the pre-dive checklist. This is particularly important because in the heat of an operation even experienced dive team members can forget simple procedures. The pre-dive checklist should include the following:

1. Determine whether the operation is in Rescue Mode or in Recovery Mode.
2. Record the diver's starting PSI.
3. Establish the minimum PSI the diver is allowed before being required to surface or end the dive.
4. Determine the maximum depth in which the pattern will be run, and maximum bottom time in reference to decompression tables.
5. Review all line signals.
6. Review the procedure for a diver in need of help.
7. Review procedure for a found object.

---

line tender will systematically examine the diver's equipment from head to toe to insure that all equipment is complete, in place and correctly fitted.

The Diver

While running search patterns, the diver functions almost like a machine. Every command comes from the line tender. The diver, in effect, becomes the line tender's senses underwater. His primary goal is to locate the object of the underwater search.

The diver's responsibilities include taking care not to disturb possible evidence, staying close to the bottom contour, making a conscientious search with one hand while holding the line in the other thus maintaining contact with the line tender.

Once the object of the search is found, the diver takes the initiative. He signals the line tender that he has found the object, and follows the subsequent procedures for that particular operation as reviewed during the predive check. At all times, the diver must take care to keep the tension in the searchline. Should he let the line go slack, he could become disoriented and have to begin the search over again.

One Diver vs. Two Divers

The buddy system is one of the most effective safe diving practices in existence. However, in most situations in rescue and recovery, one diver down can operate more effectively, and thus more safely. In such situations a backup, or safety diver, must be fully prepared, mentally and physically, to enter the water the moment assistance is requested.

The benefits of one diver down systems are that the diver does not have to relay information to his buddy, nor be concerned for his buddy's welfare, and thus has more maneuverability to make turns and stop for periodic checks of terrain, objects or other conditions.

In short, one diver can usually cover more territory in less time than two divers on the same line. There are some situations where two divers on the same line may be deemed beneficial. In a body recovery operation, for example, an inexperienced diver may need the support of the other diver.

Keep in mind, however, that in zero visibility the entangled diver is usually going to have to solve his own problem — buddy or no buddy. Also, when two divers become involved in an entanglement situation together, it just doubles the problem rather than halves it.

There are operations where dive team protocol calls for the use of two divers. A vehicle-in-the-water accident in Rescue Mode, for example, often requires that one diver check the condition of the victims, and extricate them if possible, while the other diver attaches the vehicle to a tow line. However, each diver in such an operation will usually be on a separate line, each with a separate tender and backup diver.

The Safety Diver

At all times during an operation, a safety diver must be available in the event a diver runs into trouble. Should the diver down (the primary diver) signal for help, the safety diver should already be suited up and ready to follow the line down to aid him. The safety diver must always be at the water's edge (or in the boat) next to the line tender, ready to respond immediately.

While the primary diver is swimming his search pattern, the safety diver is suited up (fins, weight belt, knife) with mask and regulator in hand. The safety diver must be an experienced diver who works well under pressure as the need for his services usually means there is trouble.

As with the decision to use one or two divers to run a pattern, the availability of a safety diver is often determined by the Risk/Benefit Factor in each situation. Only in extreme situations, such as a rescue where there is a very good chance of saving a life without creating an unreasonable risk to the potential rescuer, is the diver justified in diving without a safety diver. In Rescue Mode with two divers running patterns, one diver can be summoned to the surface and redirected to the aid of the other primary diver.

Changing Directions While Running a Pattern

The diver makes turns in the search pattern when the line tender signals that the end of a sweep or rotation has been completed. As the diver swims, he should be carrying the line in his inside hand (the hand closest to the line tender).

When the diver stops, he changes hands on the line and turns to the inside. The line tender then feeds the diver the line needed to make the next pass as the diver proceeds in the new direction. The line tender keeps good tension in the line. This prevents slack in the line which could completely disorient or entangle the diver.

When two divers are running a pattern together, the inside diver holds the line in his inside hand while the outside diver maintains contact with the inside diver by holding onto a convenient point such as the inside of his buddy's BC. The tender gives the signal and both divers stop (the signal is relayed to the outside diver by the inside diver).

As the inside diver makes the turn towards the inside, the outside diver maintains contact with him but stays outside of the turn. The outside diver must take caution not to hinder the inside diver's movements. Before moving on, the inside diver makes sure his buddy is with him and ready to continue.

Obviously, this system is more complex and leaves more room for confusion than the one diver down system.

Overlap

The two major factors determining the amount of overlap used in a pattern are visibility and the size of the object of the search. The line tender regulates the degree of overlap in the search pattern.

In zero visibility, the search pattern will have to be tight with a good degree of overlap. In clearer conditions, less overlap may be needed. However, some degree of overlap is usually necessary to ensure a thorough search. While looking for a small object, such as a handgun, the line tender may have the diver double back over the area covered on each sweep.

Knot Tying

When the diver enters the water, the line tender ties a small loop in the line to mark where the pattern began. As each pass is completed, the line tender ties a figure-8 knot in the line, marking the distance that the diver is covering. Do not use a slip knot or any type of knot that will come undone when tension is put on the line. The diver holds the line by the figure-8 knot which is tied at his end of the line. It is important that the diver be able to release the line at any time in the event the line becomes entangled.

Found Object

When the object is found, the diver signals the line tender with the predetermined three tugs. The diver then ties the line off to the object (body, evidence, auto, etc.). Exceptions to this are a victim in a Rescue Mode operation or evidence that could be moved by the line, such as a gun.

The diver then follows the protocol for each particular situation. The procedures following the finding of the object of an underwater search must be discussed during the predive checklist among the line tender, the primary diver and the safety diver.

When the line tender receives the found object signal from his diver, he relays the message to the team leader. The line tender then ties a double knot in the line, which can be used as a topside measurement after the recovery has been completed, and takes a compass reading off the line. All this information must be included in the line tender's final report of the operation.

The importance of the scene sketch, as described in the previous chapter, becomes apparent when documenting the procedure once the object of the search is located. Measurements, reference points and other information will prove invaluable in the event that additional evidence or information is required.

Often, a team of police divers will find themselves going back to an area where something was recovered (i.e. a stolen vehicle or a murder victim's body) to seek additional evidence. At times like those, the detailed scene sketch proves to be well worth the initial effort.

Summary

Without a specific and controlled pattern, the dive team is only performing a haphazard search. The dive team's cohesiveness is demonstrated during the execution of a search pattern. It is crucial that dive team members follow the procedures spelled out in this chapter.

However, while running search patterns, the dive team must always remain open and adaptable to new information. The efficiency of the pattern, diver-tender communications, documentation of progress, and other aspects of the search rely heavily upon the dive team's ability to operate as one coordinated unit.

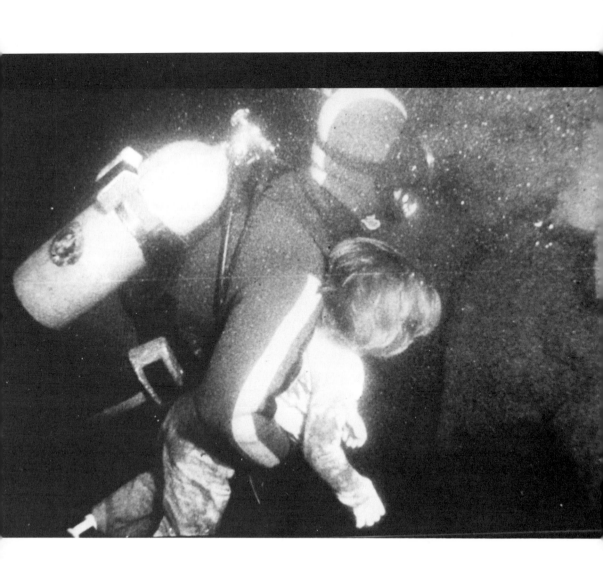

VICTIM RETRIEVAL

Dive team procedures following the location of a victim underwater vary greatly depending upon whether the operation is in Rescue or Recovery Mode. In either situation, however, a pre-established protocol is essential. Whether the objective of an operation is to save a life or to investigate a death, the manner in which it is carried out often can have an impact for years to come. Victim retrieval is virtually always accompanied with stress placed upon all parties concerned. The Dive Rescue Specialist must realize, and prepare for, the psychological effects inherent in these types of operations.

Rescue Mode
Victim Retrieval

Prior to diving, the rescue diver and his or her line tender should quickly review the steps to take upon location of the victim:

The diver will:

• Signal the line tender with three tugs when he has found and secured a grip of the victim.

• Follow the bottom contour back to shore if operating a shore-based search.

• Swim directly to the boat if operating a boat-based pattern.

The line tender will:

• Tie a knot in the line.
• Advise the team leader of the find.
• Note reference points (landmarks and/or compass headings).
• Keep slack out of the line to help the diver navigate back to surface, or (if the diver had requested it in advance), the line tender may pull the diver back to the surface.
• Alert the rest of the dive team to standby for the resuscitation procedure.

The diver should maintain a solid grasp of the victim such as under the arms and around the chest or by the belt or back of the pants. The diver must take care not to cause the victim further harm, such as by letting the victim's face drag along the bottom contour. The diver follows the bottom contour back in a shore-based search because it will be much simpler, thus faster, to relocate the victim should the diver lose contact with him. The diver's primary objective is to deliver the victim to a hard surface topside for the CPR efforts.

Resuscitation

In the rescue mode the need for inter-agency cooperation is more critical than ever. The dive team that has made advance preparations will know who to contact and/or how to accommodate the medical professionals needed for the best possible resuscitation of the victim.

Note: There is a dangerous fallacy emerging in some situations to the effect that if CPR-qualified personnel are not at the scene, it is better to leave the victim in the water (because the mammalian diving reflex is still in effect).

As stated in Chapter One, the quality of CPR administered to the victim can be a determining factor in the victim's chances for survival. Therefore, all dive team members should have CPR skills, but the ideal situation is to have professional paramedics, who are specialists in emergency medicine, perform the actual resuscitation.

Currently, an increasing number of dive teams are having professional EMTs and paramedics join their ranks. During an operation, the dive team leader may elect to keep at least one team member with advanced CPR skills topside to aid in the resuscitation.

In some unusual circumstances, the diver may have to initiate in-water CPR. Such situations are when a diver has surfaced with a victim far from shore or any watercraft. In-water CPR, however, is not as effective as CPR conducted on shore or in a boat and should only be used as a last resort.

Resuscitation on Shore

Vigorous and immediate resuscitation efforts must begin immediately upon bringing the victim to shore. Attempts should be made to preserve the victim's dignity during resuscitation efforts. Often, crowd control can be a problem. Ideally, uniformed officers should be at the scene to clear the area during resuscitation efforts. When this isn't possible, three or four team members can form a shield with blankets while facing out.

Preserving the victim's dignity is a consideration, particularly in the case of a female where the paramedics have to bare the victim's chest. Privacy measures also help the rescuers to work with a minimum of distraction.

Resuscitation in a Boat

In some circumstances the dive team may have to transport the retrieved victim to shore by boat. Resuscitation should begin in the boat. Medical personnel, or dive team members designated to begin CPR, should be present in the boat when the search is being conducted. If possible, the victim should be placed in a balanced part of the craft where the rescuers have good access to the victim.

Recovery Mode

A recovery mode operation, or body recovery, requires an entirely different approach than a rescue mode operation. The rule of thumb applied in most cases is that if the victim has been underwater for more than an hour, there is no chance for resuscitation and thus the operation is one of recovery vs. rescue.

The dive team will have to set its own time frame for making the rescue/recovery mode distinction, however, as there have been cases when a pulse has been achieved from a victim underwater as long as 60 minutes. As detailed in Chapter One, such factors as the cleanliness of the water, water temperature and the victim's age should be also taken into consideration.

As mentioned earlier, the shifting of an operation from rescue to recovery mode should be made discreetly for the sake of family, friends and bystanders. However, there should be no question among team members and members of other related agencies at the scene which mode the operation is in. Otherwise, serious confusion could result.

Locating the Body

The slower pace of a recovery operation not only provides for the safety of the divers working the operation but also allows for greater attention to detail in the investigation of the scene. Measurements, sketches and all pertinent information are compiled and automatically treated in a Recovery Mode operation as they would be in a crime scene investigation.

Though the pace is slower, the Recovery Mode operation also requires that the diver, backup diver and line tender are all thoroughly briefed in the following procedures during the predive checklist:

The diver will:
• Signal the line tender with three-tugs.
• Tie the searchline off to the body in a manner that will minimize damage to the body.
• Conduct an area search by hand for additional evidence near the body.
• Return to surface to review the strategy for recovering the body.
• Conduct a complete investigation (with photography if possible), of the underwater scene, body's positioning and condition underwater.
• In some cases, wait for a second diver to bring down a body bag or evidence containers instead of retrieving the body singlehandedly.

The line tender will:
• Tie a double knot in the line.
• Maintain contact with the line as the diver makes a hand search of the immediate area for additional evidence.

• Take a compass reading off the line, make note of it in his record book, and tie a double knot in the searchline.
• Keep line taut as the diver follows it back (with one end tied to the body) to report topside. Note: The line tender must be careful not to pull or change the location of the victim's body through this tension.

Removing the Body

When to remove the body depends upon the established procedures of that particular community. In many places, a body should not be removed from the water until the approval of the medical examiner or coroner has been given. It is often advantageous in these situations to wait for the arrival of the coroner before surfacing the body. The dive team will want to avoid having the body topside at the scene for an extended period while waiting for the coroner to show up.

Note: When moving the body off the bottom contour, be sure to check the area beneath the victim for additional evidence.

As mentioned in Chapter Four, the family should be removed from the scene and precautions taken to avoid explicit photo or television coverage. If necessary, the body can be transported by boat to another location, away from the crowd and press. If the dive team cannot avoid removing the body from the water in front of the cameras, they should have as many people as possible carrying the body, shielding it from sight. The general rule of consideration is to handle the body as if it were your relative.

Bagging the Body Underwater

Whenever possible, the body should be bagged underwater. Body bags designed especially for this purpose are available with screen mesh panels for water drainage. A conventional body bag is not practical for this purpose because of the weight of the water which would become trapped during bagging the body underwater.

In the event of suspicious circumstances, the hands should be bagged individually with plastic bags, extending to the elbows, and secured with bands at those points. Despite the condition of the body found underwater, fingernail scrapings could yield evidence, just as in a topside investigation. When bagging the hands underwater, be cautious when surfacing the victim that water trapped in those bags does not cause the bags to fall off.

The searchline tied off to the body should remain attached to the victim even after bagging. In the event the body is dropped, it could then be quickly retrieved again. Often, it is easier to refloat the body with a small lift bag than to pull the body along the bottom contour.

Post Mortem Observation

Determining the cause of death is officially the job of the medical examiner or coroner. However, professional dive team members must be aware of the variety and range of conditions involved with death in the water. Dive team members often must testify about the condition of a recovered body. However, while the Dive Rescue Specialist's observations can be important, he must be aware of his limitations in this area and refrain from drawing his own conclusions.

Likewise, the Dive Rescue Specialist must appreciate the futility in attempting to predict body refloat. By spelling out the factors which can affect body refloat, the dive team liaison to the surviving family, the press and

other agencies can better explain the difficulties of accurate predictions.

Dive Rescue Specialists would be wise to consider their limited knowledge in this area as background, rather than expertise. It is the dive team's job to report what it has observed leaving interpretation and conclusions to the pathologists.

Conditions of the Body Found in Water

Positioning

Often the body of a drowning victim will be found in a prone, semi-fetal position. At times, the body's position in the water may cause post mortem wounds and abrasions. Viewing the body, the diver will want to check and see if the body is entangled, or contorted in the position in which it was found. Hands often are significant. Note whether the victim is, or had been, clutching anything. Again, such observations must be documented.

Rigor Mortis

Rigor mortis, the stiffening of the muscle tissue after death, is caused by the buildup of lactic acid in the muscles. This condition will vary with the time that has elapsed since death and the water temperature.

Depending upon such conditions as ambient temperature, rigor mortis does cease eventually and the muscles become lucid again. In the event that a body must in some way be manipulated to fit into the body bag because of rigor mortis, the procedure used should be noted in the dive team documentation of the recovery operation.

Rigor Mortis will be more pronounced sooner in a victim that made a violent struggle prior to death — such activity generates lactic acid. In some cases, a rare phenomena of instantaneous rigor mortis, cadaveric spasm, may affect a specific part of the body such as the hand and arm of a victim who clutched an object in the throes of death.

Algor Mortis

Algor Mortis is the cooling of the body temperature. After death, a body in the water normally cools at the rate of 1.5 degrees Fahrenheit per hour. This cooling is subject to many variables including body fat, ambient temperature and the victim's clothing.

Post Mortem Lividity

Soon after death, the blood will settle into the lowest points of the body. In other words, if the body were to lay face down immediately after death, this condition will appear on the anterior portions, if face up then it appears on the posterior portions.

Post mortem lividity is the cooling and settling of blood and is denoted by splotches of pink or reddish coloring. This configuration is more pronounced in topside deaths — lividity in victims found in the water is reduced by the buoyancy in water.

However, should post mortem lividity be observed in a section that is not one of the closest to the bottom contour (i.e. it appears on the forehead of a victim laying face-up) then the condition may indicate the body was put underwater after death occurred. In such instances, written documentation of such an observance is critical as it could involve a crime situation.

Trauma

Wounds or obvious injuries may often have been contributing, if not major, causes of death of the victim found underwater. A wound received at least minutes prior to death will normally display more blood than one received at the moment of death or

afterwards. Documentation of blood evidence is therefore critical in many cases.

Conditions Affecting Body Refloat

There are a number of factors which will affect when, if at all, the body will resurface. Once a body sinks, it will go all the way to the bottom (despite many beliefs to the contrary). Likewise, once the body begins to float, it will come all the way back to the surface.

Body refloating is caused by the buoyancy of the gasses trapped within the body. The major cause of body refloat is internal decomposition, particularly as it creates a gas buildup trapped in the victim's intestinal tract.

Water Temperature

Decomposition, the disintegration of the body's soft tissues, is the primary factor in body refloat: The faster the decomposition process occurs, the sooner the body is likely to refloat. Water temperature is the major factor affecting decomposition of the body. Generally, the process will occur in the body unless the body's internal temperature drops (algor mortis) to 38 degrees Fahrenheit or less (the cooler temperatures inhibit bacterial growth necessary for decomposition and subsequent gas buildup). Also, gasses will diffuse into cool water more rapidly than in warmer water, a factor which also inhibits refloat because of the limited gas buildup.

Depth

Normally, deeper water is cooler than the water closer to the surface. The gasses created by the body will diffuse into the water much more quickly in cooler waters, thus decreasing the internal gas buildup needed for refloat. Also, the greater the

Additional factors which can contribute to body refloat are:

Type of Water — Water condition will also affect the rate of decomposition — clean water is less conducive to decomposition than murky waters. The more bacteria in the water, the faster will be the decomposition and the subsequent gas buildup in the body.

Marine Life — Particularly in salt water, marine life feeding upon a body can affect its buoyancy. In some instances, the feeding of marine life upon a body can prevent refloat entirely.

Clothing — What the victim was wearing can often promote or inhibit buoyancy. In some case, clothing will also limit the foraging of marine life.

Mode of Death — Trauma caused by wounding, open gashes and such injuries could cause a body to decompose faster than those with no trauma. However, open wounds could also make it more difficult for the internal gas buildup needed for refloat to occur.

Recent Food Eaten — A victim who hasn't eaten anything hours before death will take longer to produce the gasses necessary for refloat than the victim that did eat. Also, a high carbohydrate meal, such as beer and chili, will contribute to gas production more than a lighter diet.

depth the greater the degree of pressure which limits the buoyancy of the gasses that do accumulate within the body. Depth, therefore, creates a double negative situation for inhibiting refloat.

In some cases, depth can prevent a body from refloating at all. It should be noted, however, that if a slight amount of buoyancy can be achieved by the body's gas buildup, then the body is certain to float back to the surface as the pressure against the gasses will continually decrease as the body proceeds upward. This exponential increase often causes the body to travel upward at an accelerated rate by the time it reaches the surface.

However, once the body is on the surface it can sink again after gasses escape from the body. The length of time for the body to resink depends upon a myriad of conditions as is the case with refloat. There are cases where a body will refloat again a second time (another phenomena relying upon a wide range of conditions).

The variables affecting refloat must be weighed differently in each situation. Predicting when a body will refloat with any accuracy is extremely difficult, yet dive team members are frequently asked to do so. Assessing such situations is difficult and often the best a Dive Rescue Specialist can do is to explain this difficulty.

Summary

Victim retrieval is an area of underwater operations that can give the dive team and its members the greatest personal satisfaction. An increasing number of lives are being saved each year by dive teams using efficient underwater search and rescue techniques.

However, victim retrieval operations are often the most demanding, both physically and emotionally, for the professional dive team. Whether human lives or dignity are affected, it is the dive team that sits under public scrutiny during such operations. A well-executed operation will reflect directly upon the team's image in its community.

VEHICLE ACCIDENTS

Dive teams everywhere are being called to an increasing number of vehicle-in-the-water accidents. Such operations require special precautions and techniques for the dive team. As with victim retrieval, these operations vary greatly, depending upon whether they are being run in Rescue or Recovery Mode. Often, it is not known how many, if any at all, victims are involved until the vehicle is removed from the water.

Familiarity and skill with the techniques used to make rescues, recoveries and investigations for the auto accident operation enable the dive team to work expeditiously while remaining adaptable to changing conditions.

Responding to the Vehicle Accident in Rescue Mode

As with any call for a victim underwater, the one hour of immersion is the general rule of thumb for determining whether an operation is run in rescue or recovery mode.

A rapid scene evaluation must be made to direct the diver(s) to a good last-seen-point in a vehicle-in-the-water accident, just as in any other rescue operation.

In addition to information from eyewit-

nesses, the dive team should look for tire tracks and possible debris from the wreckage on shore leading to the water. Damage to natural or man-made structures, such as trees or guard rails, and skid marks are often helpful clues to the vehicle's location.

Such conditions are also good indicators as to what the victim's condition will be — a factor which helps to determine whether the operation should be conducted in Rescue or Recovery Mode.

Air bubbles (shortly after an accident) or a gas and oil slick on the surface often are good markings of a vehicle's location — they are also a good indicator that the vehicle has not been underwater for an extended period of time.

An evaluation of the accident scene, and, when possible, the vehicle's condition, can be good indicators of the victim's chances of survival. According to some medical experts, the additional trauma a victim is likely to suffer in an auto accident, as opposed to a simple drowning, greatly reduces the victim's chances for survival through the cold-water near-drowning phenomena. Once again, the Risk/Benefit Factor plays a primary role in the operational plan.

A tow truck often plays an essential role in

an underwater operation. The dive team is well-advised to train in advance with a local tow truck operator. Not only do the divers gain valuable experience, but also the tow truck operator receives an orientation to the need for his services during a vehicle-in-the-water accident.

Sometimes the size of a tow truck is important. If the accident involves a heavy truck or bus then the dive team will need to summon an appropriately-sized tow truck. In Rescue Mode, the tow truck should automatically be called to the scene.

Should the dive team decide to operate in the Rescue Mode, every second is used with the single objective of removing the victims from the water. The dive team leader may decide to save time by having the victims taken from the vehicle prior to removing it from the water.

The team leader, however, may want to leave the ultimate decision to his divers who will make firsthand observations underwater. Such factors as jammed doors and trapped victims may dictate the need to surface the vehicle before extracting the victims.

Note: A high percentage of dive teams are comprised of firefighters and other professionals who have experience with, and accessibility to, such high-powered extraction tools as the Hurst Tool. However, while this type of equipment is often guaranteed to work underwater, it would be unwise to employ them. Even if the diver has experience with such equipment, in conditions such as zero visibility it can be impossible to see what one is cutting or prying on. Control of these types of tools can be very difficult underwater.

Upon locating the vehicle underwater, the

diver should make certain that a victim was not thrown out, or managed to escape the vehicle before taking on water. There have been cases where victims have been found underwater as far as 40 feet from the vehicle although they were inside the vehicle when it entered the water.

The Air Pocket Myth

A common misconception about cases where vehicles are totally submerged in water is the possibility of air pockets in which the victims may be surviving. While air pockets are not impossible, they are much less likely than is generally believed. Thanks to the imaginations of novelists and Hollywood scriptwriters, many people think that air pockets are a consistent phenomena regarding submerged vehicles.

However, experiments with vehicles purposefully submerged in water have shown that a vehicle usually loses all air retaining capabilities as soon as it goes underwater. In real life situations the chances of an air pocket are decreased by such factors as

carpet and head liners floating around, damage to the vehicle's body, floating debris, etc. Thus, a potential air pocket should not be a consideration when the dive team is determining whether or not to operate in the Rescue Mode.

Most vehicles will float momentarily (40 seconds to one minute) prior to sinking. A vehicle floating and then sinking into water deeper than the vehicle's length often will flip onto the roof in the "turn turtle" position. An upside down vehicle can be disorienting to the diver who is surveying or penetrating the situation.

Badly damaged vehicles present a hazard to divers in the form of jagged, razor-sharp edges. This is a particular problem in situations where a current is present and a diver could easily be washed against the vehicle. Always approach a submerged vehicle from the downstream side when dealing with a current.

Many vehicle accidents result with the vehicle submerged in a ditch or canal. In such cases, the initial search may be done with topside personnel probing with pike

---

On The Scene

Risk/Benefit

A sports car traveling at a high rate of speed went out of control, left the road and crashed into the middle of a rapid river. The accident occurred in the spring run-off when the river's force was at its peak.

The responding dive team viewed the mangled wreckage from the bank and determined that the driver, and any possible passengers, could not still be inside

the vehicle. The extensive damage to the car showed little hope of survivors.

Considering the force of the swift water, the vehicle's condition, and the absence of a good last-seen-point, the team leader decided that the ultimate possible benefit of finding the bodies did not merit the risk of injury or death to his divers. This operation was aborted because, in short, the risk clearly outweighed the benefit.

poles. During such operations it is wise to position other shore personnel downstream to watch for floating victims, debris or other evidence. It is unlikely, however, that the vehicle itself will be moved by most currents. Usually a vehicle will be found in the spot where it went in the water.

Note: As soon as the license plate number is visible, it should be run for a listing of the owner and possible phone numbers called in an attempt to learn how many victims were in the vehicle.

The Recovery Mode Response to the Vehicle-in-the-Water Accident

As with other types of water accidents, the Recovery Mode operation is done at a much slower pace than if it were executed in Rescue Mode. Once the vehicle is located, it is desirable to have two divers verify the positioning and condition of the vehicle. Often, eventual litigation can raise the question of how much damage the vehicle received during the recovery operation.

Good quality and comprehensive underwater photographs may prove valuable in the courtroom at a later date. Photographs, in some situations, can also reveal aspects not observed by the divers firsthand. Before raising the vehicle, it is wise to photograph the surface area of the water over it. This can be accomplished from a bridge or some structure such as a snorkel truck ladder. If the vehicle cannot be seen from topside, the position should be marked for the topside photographs with a buoy.

Basically the same procedures are used to retrieve the vehicle in Recovery Mode as in Rescue Mode, but the time factor allows for a much more detailed investigation of the scene before the vehicle is removed. Divers should check to see if the vehicle's key is turned on, if the lights are on, and if the

vehicle is in gear. The divers should attempt to see if the vehicle's gas pedal has been tampered with (i.e. weighted down with a rock).

It is also wise to remove papers, documents and registration from the glove compartment, visor and/or side pouches as these could easily be washed away during the recovery.

The fingerprint potential should be protected with cautious handling of the steering wheel, rear view mirror, handles, etc. — particularly with vehicles discovered under suspicious circumstances.

Extricating the Victims

Removing the vehicle prior to victim extrication is often more practical even when there is adequate time to do otherwise. There are numerous power tools useful for victim extrication. However, as mentioned earlier, such instruments are often more time consuming and hazardous than simply refloating and/or towing the vehicle to shore so it can be worked on topside.

When determining if the vehicle should be raised first, or if the victims can be removed while it is still underwater, the diver should try the doors, reach through the windows, and make an overall survey of the vehicle's condition and position.

Divers must carefully consider the risk of entanglement before entering a vehicle — a diver should particularly avoid entering a standard or compact sized car. A trapped diver will only complicate the operation rather than help resolve it. In most modern vehicles, a diver can check the entire vehicle by simply reaching inside with an arm.

Removing the Vehicle from the Water

If victims cannot be removed from the vehicle underwater then preparations to remove the vehicle from the water should begin. The best apparatus for vehicle removal is a heavy duty, nylon webbing attachment strap. Chains and cable, though strong enough, are bulky and difficult to handle underwater. Also, tow cable will snap at times which can present a number of hazards.

Divers and all other personnel must stand clear while the vehicle is being moved. In some instances, the vehicle may be refloated with lift bags prior to towing it to shore. However, refloating objects is a special skill and requires training before attempting it.

Summary

Competent dive teams are invaluable to law enforcement agencies investigating vehicle-in-the-water accidents. Careful attention to detail and meticulous documentation help the dive team to fulfill its role. The dive team must never depend upon other agencies to do its documentation. At the scene, the vehicle's license number, nearby mile markers, and other pertinent data should be recorded in dive team reports.

A reserve plan must always be kept in mind during an operation — even after the vehicle has been located, inspected and prepared for recovery from the water. The varieties of vehicle-in-the-water accidents are virtually unlimited. Safe, efficient operations dealing with these types of conditions can only result from substantial training (with close to real life conditions) and constant research.

THE UNDERWATER INVESTIGATION

Today, law enforcement agencies throughout the world are taking advantage of contemporary underwater investigative techniques. Cases are being closed that just a few years ago would have remained unsolved indefinitely as an increasing number of weapons, bodies, vehicles and other evidence are being concealed in the water.

The manner in which the dive team handles, preserves and presents evidence found underwater can have a profound impact on a criminal investigation. When dealing with evidence, the professional dive team must keep in mind the ultimate use and destination of objects recovered and the subsequent documentation of the operation.

The dive team that serves local law enforcement officials during an investigation is assuming a professional responsibility for its role in the case. Whether a diver is a police officer, firefighter, paramedic or volunteer, he or she must perform to his or her highest potential during an underwater investigation for the sake of the public safety.

Finding Evidence

What constitutes evidence at the underwater crime scene is the decision of the law enforcement officer charged with the inves-

tigation. The divers underwater, however, will have to use discretion as they survey the bottom contour and report back to the investigator.

A good rule of thumb is that it is better to overcollect evidence than to leave anything that may be important later. It is always easier to collect evidence the first time around than it is to have to return to the scene and repeat the diving operation.

Any articles that appear to be out of place or damaged, in addition to the obvious pieces of evidence, should be collected. Virtually any object, even something as trivial as a gum wrapper, has the potential to be evidence. Also, keep in mind that it is possible to collect fingerprints off some items found underwater.

A thorough search of the area should always be made for additional evidence. For example, after a body has been found and photographed, with the relevant measurements and diagrams documented, the dive team should then make a thorough search of an area (the size of which depends upon the conditions at the scene).

At times the dive team may want to make an additional evidence search on land when topside investigators have not done so. The object of such a comprehensive search is to check for items pertinent to the death.

Documenting the Crime Scene

Before any evidence is touched, it should be photographed if possible. Exceptions to this procedure are when evidence relates to the rescue mode (i.e. the victim is entangled in rope) and must be destroyed or altered to save a life. Other exceptions are when the evidence itself is threatened by weather or other activities in the area, such as a dragging operation). Also, conditions such as zero visibility can impede the use of photography for documentation.

Photographs should be marked with the case number, the photographer's name, the location and a description of the subject of the photo. Crime scene photographs are evidence themselves and must be handled through the "chain of custody" like any other piece of evidence. Underwater photographs can often yield characteristics of a scene that are not evident firsthand, and are solid evidence in a courtroom.

All measurements, compass readings and other pertinent information are entered into the scene sketch. The scene sketch must be accurate and clear. Many times it is the scene sketch that will represent the dive team operation years later in the courtroom. There are two basic methods of making a scene sketch; the baseline method and the triangulation method.

The Baseline Method

The baseline method is used when there is a solid straight line available. A pier or boat ramp often serves this purpose. A polypropylene searchline is pegged topside, run along the structure and out into the water to a point parallel with the crime scene evi-

dence. A measurement is then taken of the evidence at a 90 degree angle from the line.

Note: It is important that the distance from shore is measured from a fixed point, such as the edge of a pier. The edge of the water will not do.

The Triangulation Method

The triangulation method employs two separate, permanent points on shore (corner of building, bridges) with measurements from each intersecting at the location of the evidence. Objects such as trees and telephone poles are not preferable because they can be damaged or moved with time.

Note: This method is commonly used with good results, but it can be difficult to remark the exact location if the points at which the lines are based were too close together, thus creating tight angles at the base of the triangle.

The Rectangular Method

This method is favored when a grid pattern sketch is needed in the documentation. To make a rectangular measurement, two stationary points on shore will be needed. Lines are run into the water from each point and parallel to one another. Equidistant measurements are taken from each line. The lines are intersected at a point beyond the scene with a line connecting the two, and bisecting them at 90 degree angles. Using the parallel lines and the connecting line as reference points, the location of the evidence is then measured and recorded.

While the rectangular method is more cumbersome than the baseline or triangulation methods of crime scene diagramming, it is ideal for situations where the investigating dive team wishes to show the relationship of the locations of different items of evidence (i.e. a gun and a body). The stationary points must be permanent fixtures such as pier pilings, street lights or bridge abutments.

Photo Leads To Conviction

The photographing of evidence underwater, combined with proper documentation of measurements, were the key elements in protecting the validity of a Canadian mass murderer's confession.

Following the suspect's confession, a Royal Canadian Mounted Police dive team searched for and found his dismantled high-powered rifle in a lake. However, the suspect's lawyers argued that their client had confessed to disposing of a rifle that had a scope. The RCMP divers had not produced a scope, just the rifle.

According to Canadian rules of evidence, there was the chance that the confession could be thrown out of court. While the divers felt they had made a thorough search of the area, they were surprised, and relieved, to discover that the underwater crime photographs contained an object that looked like a rifle scope.

"The scope was actually easier to see in the photographs than it was at the scene," recalls the RCMP dive team leader, Cpl. Bob Teather. Because they had taken care to document the distances at the scene, the RCMP divers knew exactly where to look for the rifle scope. They retrieved the missing piece of evidence and the murderer's confession was used to win a conviction.

Removing Evidence

During the removal of evidence, caution must be taken to not affect the evidentiary nature of the object(s). For example, if a body is tied to a heavy object it would be better to cut the rope rather than to untie it as the knot could be part of the suspect's method of operation. In the event that evidence needs to be altered in some way to make the retrieval, the procedure must be documented in the diver's report.

While the possibility of fingerprints is limited, there is potential for such evidence on objects found underwater. Thus, divers should be conscious of fingerprint potential when handling evidence. Limit the handling of evidence as much as possible. If evidence must be handled, try to touch it in a manner in which it's evidentiary value is least disturbed. Avoid placing objects in plastic bags which can rub off any possible fingerprints.

Preservation of Evidence

The goal of the diver collecting evidence is to keep it in the condition in which it was found. In this respect, evidence found underwater must be handled differently than topside evidence.

Clothing, fabric and particles should be placed on clean dry paper and air dried. Do not put wet fabric or paper evidence on newspaper to dry. Wet newspaper will often bleed ink onto fabric.

Also, do not use a fan to dry fabrics as particles could be blown away or other particles blown onto the evidence. Particles that fall from clothing, or other evidence, should be packaged separately and labeled before shipping to the crime lab. Do not leave wet clothing or fabric in a plastic bag. Plastic bags may be used to transport wet clothing, but they should be removed as soon as possible to avoid rot and mildew.

When retrieving wet paper, either underwater or topside, pick the paper up by the edges. It is best to use tweezers for this task if possible. If folded, carefully unfold the paper in a bucket of water. Avoid drying paper in direct sunlight which could destroy ink and pigments. Likewise, fibers of any kind should be treated gently and protected from the elements (i.e. wind). One of the major benefits of an underwater body bag is the preservation of possible fiber evidence in a criminal investigation.

Consult with the responsible crime lab technician before handling evidence. The best scenario involves the dive team and the investigating agency reviewing the evidence retrieval and handling procedures in advance.

Handling Firearms Underwater

When searching for a gun in zero visibility, pat or scrape the ground very lightly. The diver must keep in mind that a gun underwater can discharge; there are documented cases of this occurring. Extra care must also be taken to preserve potential fingerprints. The ultimate decision on how to handle a weapon found as evidence belongs to the investigator charged with the case. However, there are methods that have proven successful for the careful handling of a gun underwater.

Guns and other metal objects are highly susceptible to oxidation once removed from the water. A gun that has been immersed for several months could be in firing condition while in the water and yet 30 minutes of exposure to air could rust the weapon beyond repair. Therefore, any gun or metal object should be kept in the same liquid (water) that it was found in.

Hard objects such as firearms, which investigators hope to find fingerprints on,

Diver places a recovered weapon into an evidence container.

must be placed in hard containers rather than in soft bags or wrappings. Plastic food containers or custom-cut PVC pipe with sealable ends work well for this purpose. A gun can be scooped into one of these containers without being touched by hand.

When handling a gun do not put anything in the barrel, like a rod or pencil, as such actions could damage the chances for a good ballistics test by altering trace residues. One method of handling a gun is to lace a string through the trigger guard to avoid gripping it.

If the gun must be handled by hand, it should be touched in an area that is unlikely to provide fingerprints, such as on the knurled grips. Even a partial gun could be used for ballistics testing provided the barrel is included.

Knives and other metal objects should be treated with the same concern for their evidentiary value by the retrieving diver. A knife can be scooped up into the PVC container or picked up cautiously to minimize the damage of potential fingerprints.

Note: When scooping up either a gun, knife or some other object, take some of the bottom sand or silt with it rather than scraping the instrument itself. This way the diver will minimize the chances of destroying possible skin scrapings, blood or other evidence.

Chain of Possession

Most law officers will cite paperwork as the element that loses the greatest number of cases. Sloppy or inadequate documentation on the part of investigators often makes the difference between conviction or acquittal for many suspects. Thus, the dive team must adhere to a strict policy of careful documentation and track the chain of possession for each piece of evidence it handles.

The diver who discovers a piece of evidence must inscribe his initials and date on a section where the evidentiary value won't be affected. This is done so that the investigating diver can make a positive identification in court, which could be required months, or even years, later. It is usually best to make such inscriptions at the lab rather than underwater or by removing such evidence as a weapon from the container at the scene.

The chain of possession should be documented with a standard "chain of custody" form. Case numbers, names of investigators and any other identifications should be included in this documentation. The investigator assigned to the case is responsible to see that the evidence is properly tagged, packaged and taken to the crime lab for further examination.

Evidence is turned over to the crime lab accompanied by the laboratory request or "letter of transmittal." In critical cases, such as homicides, it is often preferable that the evidence be hand delivered to its custodians by those in charge of the investigation. It is best to keep the number of persons handling evidence to a minimum. The fewer people in the chain of possession process, the simpler the task of all those involved in the courtroom phase.

Summary

Meticulous handling of evidence is a clear demonstration of the dive team's professionalism. For many years, successful investigations were impossible when circumstances involved evidence that was discarded or lost in the water. Today, an increasing number of crime scenes involve water as the criminal element tries to avoid sophisticated topside detection devices and techniques. Proper dive team procedures in searching, combined with the skillful handling of evidence are helping to shrink the law breaker's domain.

SUMMARY

The Dive Rescue Specialist never completes the educational process. Regardless of the number and range of certifications earned, there will always be an abundance of new information, techniques and experiences with which the Dive Rescue Specialist can enhance his or her skill level.

The stakes in underwater rescue and recovery operations are too high to accommodate overconfidence. While dive team members should be able to take pride in their abilities, a realistic attitude is balanced with caution and humility.

No one is above mistakes. At times, the veteran dive team member is more susceptible than a rookie is to making a fatal error —the result of overconfidence, relaxed protocol, or a combination of both.

Each year, dive team members — both volunteers and paid personnel — suffer injuries and close calls on operations. A handful of these divers drown. The authors of this manual believe the majority of these accidents are avoidable.

The professional underwater rescue and recovery team never drops its guard. The most recent predive checklist is no less detailed than the first one. Last week's training session is as well-planned as the team's first open water dive. No piece of dive team equipment gathers dust — even if it has never been used in an operation, yet.

If you have studied this manual, and have become adept at the procedures outlined here, then you have made a good beginning. These procedures are based upon the real-world experiences of the authors. And while experience is the best teacher, preparation and knowledge will streamline that educational process.

A solid background not only helps the Dive Rescue Specialist to maximize field learning, it greatly reduces the chances for paying the tragic price that trial-and-error practices often carry.

There are many areas and specialities which will require further instruction. Depending upon a dive team's respective environment, such specialities as swiftwater rescue, hazardous materials diving, ice diving, or vertical rope tactics could merit further training.

The accomplished Dive Rescue Specialist, who is committed to the welfare of his or her community, will also become involved in dive team administration. Funding, public education and team management will require time and effort on the part of the individual members for the sake of the entire dive team.

Underwater rescue and recovery work involves many hazards, distasteful tasks, and heartbreaking experiences. But this field can also be a most rewarding one for the diver.

As a Dive Rescue Specialist, you have elected to fill a challenging role. Keep an open mind and a healthy respect for the unpredictable, and never venture into the water without attaching a Risk/Benefit Factor to *every* operation.

PHOTO CREDITS

Cover photos by Scott Hill, Bob Clark, Steve Linton, and Diving Systems International/ Steve Barsky.